The Happy Economist

THE HAPPY ECONOMIST

HAPPINESS FOR THE HARD-HEADED

Ross Gittins

ALLEN&UNWIN

First published in Australia in 2010

Allen & Unwin
83 Alexander Street
Crows Nest NSW 2065
Australia
Phone: (61 2) 8425 0100
Fax: (61 2) 9906 2218
Email: info@allenandunwin.com
Web: www.allenandunwin.com

Cataloguing-in-Publication details are available from the National Library of Australia
www.librariesaustralia.nla.gov.au

ISBN 978 1 74175 673 9

Typeset in 12.5/15 Centaur by Midland Typesetters, Maryborough
Printed and bound in Australia by McPherons's Printing Group

10 9 8 7 6 5 4 3 2 1

Contents

INTRODUCTION: HAPPINESS AND ECONOMICS

Happiness is no laughing mattter.
— Richard Whately

This is a book about happiness. It says a lot about the practical things we can do as individuals to live happier lives and about what governments could do to help us in that. But it also takes a different, harder-headed, more economics-oriented approach to the subject. Huh? What light could economics shed on the topic? Isn't it meant to be the dismal science? Sure. But actually, the question should be the other way round: what light does our eternal pursuit of happiness shed on the adequacy and relevance of the doctrines of economics, doctrines that permeate the public discussion of what governments should do and what we want out of life?

Hard though it is to believe, economics started out with the goal of helping people maximise their happiness—though the economists preferred to call it 'utility'. But economics lost its way in the 1930s. Concluding—prematurely, as it's turned out—that our utility can't be measured directly, it took the logical shortcut of assuming that studying the things we bought would reveal our preferences. Our true preferences. Economists became great believers that only what we did counted; anything we *said* about our preferences was of little reliability. Sorry, not that simple.

But you can see how this switch of focus to the things we buy led inexorably to economists occupying the place they do now: preachers of the gospel of greater efficiency so as to maximise our material consumption, high priests in the Temple of Mammon. I believe we live in an age of heightened materialism. Economists can't take all the blame for that. All of us are materialist to a greater or lesser extent, and the push to make us more so is coming from our business people—from their advertising and marketing as well as from the things they say—and from politicians of every colour save, perhaps, green. What has changed is that, in this more materialist mood, we take more notice of economists and the 'reforms' they advocate. In doing so, we've allowed them to fan the flames of our materialism.

We can see our greater materialism in the way we, as a society, have chosen to take the fruits of the ever-improving productivity of our labour in the form of higher real wages rather than shorter working hours. There was a time when governments used legislation to impose a shorter working week—or provision for long-service leave—on employers. Could you imagine a government doing that today? In the early 1980s the union movement used the arbitration system to impose a move from the 40- to a 38-hour week, but the move was so controversial at the time it probably contributed to the decline of both the union movement and the arbitration system. There's been no talk of shorter working weeks since.

We can see our greater materialism in the ease with which businesses have been able to achieve the deregulation of shopping hours and the removal of weekend and public holiday penalty rates from industrial awards. More freedom to shop, eat out and enjoy commercial entertainment on the weekend? Great. Disruption of the family lives of people now required to work at weekends while their spouse and children and friends are available for social interaction? Oh, didn't think of that.

We can see greater materialism in the decline of 'voluntary compliance' with the tax laws and the greater use of accountants and lawyers to find loopholes and minimise the tax we pay. When Australia's richest man, the late Kerry Packer, announced to a parliamentary committee his belief that only a fool would pay more tax than he could get away with, the public's response was more one of envy than disapproval.

We can see greater materialism in the way chief executives and company directors have hugely increased their salary packages over the past 20 years, despite public disapproval. If they can get away with imposing it on their shareholders now, what was stopping them doing it much earlier? The inhibitions of the chief executives of the day, which have since fallen away.

The key question—the eternally asked question—is whether money buys happiness. Most people *say* no, but *act* yes. The truth is more complicated, and this book devotes a lot of space to exploring it. As to why we say one thing and do another, the evolutionary psychologists offer the best explanation. Indeed, they provide a lot of insight into why humans behave the way they do, including why we pursue happiness with such vigour.

It should now be clear that, in this pursuit, we can't rely on much help from economics. For that we must turn to the psychologists who've led the academic study of happiness—or 'subjective wellbeing' as they prefer to call it—and the attempt to put it on a more scientific basis. They've had some help from a few enlightened economists, however, and I'll point out their contributions.

One other point of intersection between happiness and economics concerns work. Should work be seen merely as a means to an end—an unavoidable unpleasantness needed to obtain the wherewithal to sustain life and leisure—or is it possible to derive happiness from work? Some employers would see their workers' happiness as no concern of theirs, but I see it very differently and this is another key theme of the book.

But by now you may be feeling a bit uneasy. Is happiness a suitably worthy topic for someone who takes a pride in being hard-headed? Isn't the pursuit of personal happiness a rather shallow, self-centred business, preoccupied with seeking a good time, maximising pleasure and minimising pain? Doesn't it encourage smugness and a lack of concern about an unjust world? Doesn't the 'practice of contentment' act as an antidote to ambition and striving for progress? In some people's minds it may be all those things, but it doesn't have to be. My conception of happiness is much broader than that, and the book begins with a discussion of what we mean by the word.

There's little controversy over the proposition that happiness is a matter for the individual. If a person wants to pursue it that's their right and how they go about it is a matter for them provided they stay within the law. Alternatively, if happiness doesn't strike them as a worthy goal for their lives, that's their right too. The first part of the book deals with happiness at the personal level—'micro happiness', as I call it.

More controversial is the question of whether governments should get involved in promoting the happiness of their populations. Shouldn't they limit themselves to helping us in more practical ways, sticking to improving our *objective* wellbeing—our health, our education, our prosperity? I tackle these issues in part two, on 'macro happiness'. Whether or not governments *should* be seeking to maximise 'aggregate happiness' I argue that, in practice, all of them do seek to. Their problem is that, lacking appreciation of modern psychology's insights into what does and doesn't make us happy, they don't do it well. I examine the strengths and weaknesses of economics, the dominant ideology of our times, with its supreme goal of unending growth in production and consumption.

How does this square with the scientists' warnings that greenhouse gas emissions and other encroachments on the natural environment are bringing us close to 'the limits to growth'? It doesn't. But that doesn't mean the goals of economic management couldn't be re-aligned to keep us out of trouble—and, in the process, avert a lot of looming unhappiness. And if it can also be shown that economic growth doesn't lead to increased happiness, that would cast further doubt on the wisdom of its continued pursuit.

In the end, subjective wellbeing triumphs over objective wellbeing because we are what we feel. Being healthy and prosperous but feeling lousy isn't a great way to be. Truly hard-headed people understand the importance of being happy.

PART ONE
MICRO HAPPINESS

1

WHAT IS HAPPINESS?

Man meeting an economist he knows in the street: How's your wife?
Economist: Relative to what?
— Joke told by Professor Allan Fels

When I went to Sunday school in the 1950s, happiness was part of the curriculum. One of the choruses we used to sing (and spell) was:

I'm H-A-P-P-Y,
I'm H-A-P-P-Y,
I know I am, I'm sure I am,
I'm H-A-P-P-Y.

And another:

If you're happy and you know it, clap your hands.
If you're happy and you know it, clap your hands.
If you're happy and you know it,
And you really want to show it,
If you're happy and you know it, clap your hands.

Well, from where I'm sitting, a childhood in the 1950s *was* happy—especially in retrospect. Since then, however, the interest in happiness has become a lot more adult, a lot more commercialised and a lot more scientific. Dozens of popular books with the word 'happiness' in their titles have been published in the past decade. I've read a lot of them and will quote from the most authoritative. Why such a glut? Perhaps because the satisfaction of so many of our material ambitions in recent decades has, paradoxically, left us vaguely unsatisfied, or unhappy if you like. Is that all there is? Or perhaps it's that, as our material needs edge closer to satiation—a point I doubt we'll ever reach—our aspirations turn to higher order, more psychological needs.

I remember noticing that the Australian public's measured concern about environmental issues reached a peak in the economic boom of the late 1980s. With employment and wages growing strongly, we had room to worry about pollution and recycling. But as the boom turned to bust in the early 1990s, concerns about the availability of jobs and the malfunctioning of the economy seemed to crowd out concerns about the environment. I formed the view then that, like so many other things, the public's degree of interest in the environment varied with the state of the business cycle. It was, in a sense, a luxury good. With the present conjuncture of another economic downturn and with the urgent need for concrete action to prevent climate change, that theory is about to be tested.

Similarly, it will be interesting to see whether the surge of public interest in happiness is merely a by-product of the world's long economic boom of the past decade or two and, if so, whether it survives the present severe global recession. I hope it does—because, as with the environment, I regard the pursuit of happiness as a matter of great intrinsic significance rather than a luxury—but I'm not sure it will.

The science of happiness

There is, however, another factor contributing to the wave of interest in happiness that points in the direction of the phenomenon being more permanent. It's that happiness—or 'subjective wellbeing', to give it its more academically respectable moniker—has become an object of considerable serious research by many social scientists, mainly psychologists, but also neuroscientists, economists and a few political scientists.

Many of the books on happiness—and, certainly, the most reliable—are written by these academic experts; most of the rest draw heavily on their findings. So when next you see the phrase, 'the science of happiness', don't be dubious. The doyen of these researchers, and the man who pioneered the field almost single-handedly, is Ed Diener, professor of psychology at the University of Illinois, Urbana-Champaign.

Building on the happiness research, and conferring on it greater academic respectability, is the relatively new 'positive psychology' movement, established at the instigation of Martin Seligman of the University of Pennsylvania, while he was president of the 160,000-member American Psychological Association. Martin observed that for the past half-century clinical psychology had been consumed by a single subject, mental illness, and argued that it needed as well to return to its earlier interest in nurturing talent and improving normal life. It should seek knowledge of what makes life worth living. As well as helping troubled people to raise their wellbeing from, say, minus eight to minus two, it should also help raise other people's wellbeing from plus five to plus eight. So positive psychology is 'the study of the conditions and processes that contribute to the flourishing or optimal functioning of people'. Sounds like a good idea to me.

Happiness has not been a major research interest for economists but, even so, small numbers of economists are contributing to the new science. It was an economic historian, Richard Easterlin, who first pointed to the paradox of the developed countries' ever-rising national incomes but little-changed happiness ratings. It's probably Professor Bruno Frey of the University of Zurich who's done most to draw to academic economists' attention the relevance of happiness studies to their traditional concerns.

Is the pursuit of happiness unworthy?

Even so, my religious upbringing makes me wonder about the proposition that the pursuit of happiness should be the chief object of our lives, let alone the goal of governments. Is happiness all there is to life? It seems so narrow in its vision, not to mention so smug, so 'I'm all right, Jack', so self-centred, so blind to the travails of others.

We say we want our children to be happy, and we certainly don't want them to be unhappy, but is that the full extent of our hopes for them? Say we could give them a drug or maybe hook them up to a machine that would keep them in a permanent state of pleasure and contentment. Would we do it? Very few of us would. Why not? Because it would be cheating; it wouldn't be playing the human game as it's intended to be played. It wouldn't be running the risks, or experiencing the joys, that come from our interactions with other people. It would involve no challenge—no learning from experience, no triumphing over adversity—and thus no feelings of satisfaction from achievement. It would be a life lived without striving, without accomplishment, without any contribution to making the world a better place.

In Aldous Huxley's novel *Brave New World*, everyone exists in ignorant bliss thanks to the drug Soma. The Controller explains that, 'universal happiness has been achieved by shifting the emphasis away from truth and beauty and towards comfort . . . Art and science have become impossible because they require challenge, skill and frustration. Happiness has got to be paid for somehow and a guarantee of comfort requires losing other experiences that are part of being human,' the Controller says.

But one person objects: 'I don't want comfort, I want God. I want poetry, I want real danger, I want freedom, I want goodness, I want sin.'

'In fact,' says the Controller, 'you're claiming the right to be unhappy.'

There has to be a place in our lives for sadness. It would be inhuman not to feel sad over the death of a loved one, the breakup of a relationship or the loss of your job. We don't want to stigmatise sadness, put a social prohibition on it, treat it as a disease or label it pathological. And never forget, sadness or frustration make us appreciate happiness when it comes.

So, is that what the present obsession with happiness amounts to—an unthinking, self-centred desire to feel good at all times? To some people it may. But it doesn't have to be and, certainly, to me happiness means a lot more than that. The word 'happiness' has a range of meanings. In its narrowest conception—the one focused on by those people with doubts about the legitimacy of happiness as a personal or public policy goal—happiness involves the constant seeking of pleasure and avoidance of pain. The better word for it is hedonism.

Levels of happiness

But to the scientists who study happiness, it comes in at least two parts. Raj Persaud, a consultant psychiatrist, says psychologists dissect happiness into two components, referred to as level 1 and level 2. Level 1 happiness is the kind of hedonistic pleasure you get from a nice glass of wine, seeing a nice film, having a nice meal. It's a pleasurable feeling state that tends to be rather intense, but also tends to be temporary. Psychologists' attempts to measure how long it lasts suggest about 15 minutes.

Level 2 happiness, on the other hand, is more cognitive or intellectual. It's the satisfaction and contentment you feel when you look at your life and think about past achievements and the general direction your life is heading in. This form of happiness is less intense than level 1 happiness, he says, but is longer lasting. Note that the two levels are frequently in conflict with each other. If you pursue too much level 1 happiness you won't get to achieve much level 2 happiness. But if you dedicate your life purely to level 2 happiness you won't have much fun.

Most scientists take 'happiness' to cover both senses and use the word interchangeably with 'subjective wellbeing' or just 'wellbeing'. Sonja Lyubomirsky, professor of psychology at the University of California, Riverside and author of *The How of Happiness*, says: 'I use the term happiness to refer to the experience of joy, contentment or positive wellbeing, combined with a sense that one's life is good, meaningful and worthwhile.' I suspect, however, that in practice what scientists measure when they question people about their happiness is closer to level 2. Bob Cummins, professor of psychology at Deakin University and supervisor of Australia's primary measure of happiness, the Australian Unity Wellbeing Index, says the happiness he focuses on 'is a mood, rather than an emotion . . . Whereas emotions are fleeting, moods are more stable', he says. 'They represent a deep feeling state which is constantly present even if we lose contact with it sometimes.'

Although all of us have done our share of seeking pleasure and avoiding pain, it's a mistake to imagine the world would be a better place if we could stamp out all negative emotions. Psychologists explain that humans have evolved to feel negative emotions for good reason. Ed Diener and his academic son Robert Biswas-Diener have written the most authoritative popular guide to the discoveries of happiness science, *Happiness: Unlocking the Mysteries of Psychological Wealth*. 'Don't be concerned if you experience sporadic anger, sadness or worry,' the Dieners say. 'Happiness is not the total absence of negative emotions. Brief feelings of sadness and guilt, while unpleasant to experience, can serve important purposes and help us function effectively.'

Our feelings help us interpret the quality of our lives and the world around us, and motivate us to behave accordingly. Fear, for instance, functions to keep us safe by motivating us to avoid perceived dangers. Guilt functions to guide our behaviour through moral decision-making, and thus helps preserve harmony in families and communities. 'Imagine how dysfunctional the world would be if people did not grieve for their deceased loved ones, feel pangs of guilt when they cheated on tests, or become angry when they were treated unjustly,' they say.

When we look at happiness as discussed by Aristotle and the ancient philosophers we leave hedonism—the mere satisfying of appetites, a life suitable to the beasts—far behind and rise to the heights of 'eudaimonia', living the good life in both senses of the word: good in that it's virtuous, aimed at making the world a better place, and good in that it's deeply satisfying. Aristotle's question was: How should we live? He saw it as the fundamental question of human existence, involving the formulation of an ethical doctrine about what constitutes a well-lived life.

Whereas hedonic enjoyment focuses on a specific *outcome*—the intense but brief feelings of pleasure for pleasure's sake—eudaimonia focuses on the *content* of your life and the *processes* involved in living well. Living well means pursuing the right ends, with satisfaction or happiness following as a mere by-product. Whereas hedonism emphasises quantity—maximising pleasant feelings—eudaimonia emphasises quality. It's about making your life meaningful, both in terms of your relationships with others and in terms of the work you do. It's also about growth—growth towards the best that is within us. Here, of course, we see plenty of scope for striving and ambition, as long as our ambition drives us towards worthy ends. The eudaimonic life is often described as 'thriving' or 'flourishing'—fulfilling your potential.

One man who's had a great influence on my thinking is Michael Schluter, founder of Britain's Relationships Foundation and patron of the Relationships Forum Australia. While almost no one would doubt that our relationships with our spouse, children, parents, siblings, other relatives, neighbours and workmates are the most important dimension of our lives, Michael's simple but profound point is that, in practice, we're always neglecting to take account of those relationships in our pursuit of other goals. His mission is to remind individuals and governments to consider the 'relational' implications of everything they do.

In *Thriving Lives*, the Relationships Foundation's response to the British public's recent preoccupation with happiness, Michael and his colleagues argue that: 'At a personal level, promoting the maxim that pleasure is good and pain is bad runs the risk of encouraging individualism, selfishness and an unhealthy focus on present experience that can be damaging over the long-term. It can too easily be used to justify risky sexual behaviours, men walking out on their families or the refusal to care for disabled or elderly relatives. It may also encourage the avoidance of any good form of pain in the way of challenge or difficult experience that is necessary for personal development and maturity.'

So they argue that both the hedonic and eudaimonic dimensions must be involved in any definition and promotion of wellbeing. 'The hedonic feelings of happiness are certainly an important part of life. But without the eudaimonic dimension, the pursuit of hedonic happiness can quickly become irresponsible and, ironically, may ultimately undermine the happiness of self and others.

'By complementing pleasure with the concept of flourishing, we've taken a step closer to gaining a better understanding of wellbeing and the goals for life. But there is one further step that needs to be taken. We do not exist as isolated individuals . . . our experience of wellbeing is deeply influenced by our connections with other people, both directly and indirectly. And when we look at wellbeing at a social level, we begin to see how much our collective wellbeing depends on choices that are not made for personal gain.'

This, they say, is most evident in direct relationships. It's certainly in the individual's long-term interest to invest in relationships, even though there may be a short-term cost. But long-term gains to yourself that are distant, uncertain and indeterminate are a poor motivation for investment in present behaviour compared to a willingness to commit to *others* and invest in their wellbeing. What's more, it's unlikely there will even be any long-term wellbeing gains from a relationship if the motivation for investment is purely one of self-interest. It's only by a genuine motivation to give without seeking personal gain that relationships flourish, they say.

Taking all that on board brings me to Martin Seligman's division of happiness into three ascending elements, in his book *Authentic Happiness*. First is the 'pleasant life'—a life of enjoyment that successfully pursues positive emotions. Second is the 'good life'—a life of engagement, in which you obtain abundant gratification in the main realms of your life. Third is the 'meaningful life'—a life of affiliation, where you use your strengths in the service of something much larger than you are, whether it be nature, social groups, organisations, movements, traditions or belief systems.

Can you make yourself happier?

A separate question is whether it's possible for us to influence our own happiness. People's scores in measurements of their happiness are so remarkably stable it has led some psychologists to the view that individuals have a genetically determined 'setpoint' for their level of happiness. This notion of 'homeostasis' draws an analogy with the control of physiological systems, such as body temperature. Our happiness may temporarily depart from its set-point, but will quickly return to it. Or maybe our happiness is held within a fairly narrow range.

Most psychologists in this field, however, see more scope for us to influence our happiness. Seligman proposes a neat formula (which I imagine would appeal to economists): $H = S + C + V$, where H is your enduring level of happiness, S is your set range, C is the circumstances of your life and V represents factors under your voluntary control. Enduring happiness is how satisfied you feel about your life—the main definition of happiness that surveys attempt to measure—as opposed to your momentary happiness after you've eaten a chocolate or lack thereof after you've had someone shout at you.

Studies of identical twins raised apart have convinced psychologists the greater part of our happiness is inherited from our parents and that happiness is, indeed, one of the most heritable aspects of personality. This is what determines each person's set range. But then there are the circumstances of our lives—our race, gender, age, marital status, education, employment, place of living, and so forth. As you see, only some of those can we change. And even when we can, it's often not easy.

That's the bad news. The good news is that, as Sonja Lyubomirsky summarises the research findings, the set-point accounts for no more than about 50 per cent of the differences in people's happiness levels, while circumstances account for as little as 10 per cent. That leaves a whole 40 per cent open to our control through intentional, voluntary activity. Phew. That's a relief.

Throughout this book I'll be quoting results from many surveys of people's happiness, most of which ask them to rate how satisfied they feel with their lives on a scale. Take the highly pertinent case of the Australian Unity Wellbeing Index. The *personal* wellbeing component of the index involves regularly asking a national sample of about 2000 adults how satisfied they feel about eight aspects of personal life—health, personal relationships, safety, standard of living, achievements, community connectedness, future security and spirituality. Respondents are asked to assess each aspect on a scale of zero to ten, where zero represents completely dissatisfied and ten represents completely satisfied. In Western countries, the average value of satisfaction from population samples is about 75 per cent, with a normal range from 70 to 80 per cent.

The question is, how reliable are such survey results? People's feelings about their subjective wellbeing are, obviously, completely subjective. So how reliable are the answers they give? How well do people understand their feelings? How honest are they about how they feel? How much are their answers affected by momentary feelings of pleasure or pain at the time they were being surveyed? That is, how consistent are people's answers?

According to the psychologists, their survey results *can* be relied upon. Sonja Lyubomirsky says studies show significant convergence between a person's self-reported wellbeing and how their spouse and their peers rate the person's happiness. Studies comparing self-reported wellbeing with people's ability to recall particular types of events tend to confirm the accuracy of their reports. Then there's the smile test. Experts can tell when our smiles are genuine (using eye muscles) or forced (using just the mouth). People who are happy smile more than others, and studies show a high correlation between how happy people claim to be and how much they smile. People's self-reports also tally roughly with what electrodes planted on their scalp reveal about electrical activity in those parts of the brain known to deal with happy feelings.

Let's try to pull this together. Happiness can be defined narrowly or broadly. If you doubt the worthiness of happiness as narrowly defined—hedonism—that's fine. So do I. But that doesn't mean you're not pursuing happiness. Sonja Lyubomirsky says: 'All of us want to be happy, even if we don't admit it openly or choose to cloak our desire in different words. Whether our dreams are about professional success, spiritual fulfilment, a sense of connection, a purpose in life, or love and sex, we covet those things because ultimately we believe that they will make us happier.'

That's what all of us are looking for, but how can we tell if what we're doing is working? What does being a happy person feel like? The Dieners say: 'We recommend that people think of happiness in terms of mildly pleasant emotions that are felt most of the time, with intense positive emotions being felt occasionally. If you feel fairly energetic and upbeat most of the time on most days, and are generally satisfied with your life with only the occasional complaint, you are, by our definition, happy.'

But, the Dieners add: 'To have the highest quality of life, you must live a life full of meaning, values, purpose, and strong social connections: a life filled primarily with positive emotions, including the spiritual emotions, such as love and gratitude, with occasional negative emotions in situations where they are helpful; a life built around activities in which you enjoy working toward your values.'

That's what I'm on about. It puts economics and the economic aspects of our lives into their proper context—important, but not worthy of the dominance many people accord them. And too likely to lead us to the blinkered pursuit of hedonism, whereas a focus on eudaimonia would be more satisfying.

We need to move on to the nitty-gritty of happiness, but first we should see what light our evolutionary history can throw on our pursuit of it. Short answer: a lot.

2

EVOLUTION AND HAPPINESS

Economics: the science of human behaviour that manages with
scientific precision to avoid any understanding of humans.
— David James, *The Business Devil's Dictionary*

How much do you know about evolution? If you're like most
people, a bit but not a lot. It's worth knowing more
because the exploration of natural selection to improve our
understanding of why humans work the way they do is probably
the most interesting recent development in the social sciences.
Evolution can be used to explain why we strive to be happy and
why we find so many aspects of modern life a bit of a struggle.
It also reveals some of the limitations of conventional economics and explains our susceptibility to materialism. Much of this
has to do with the evolution of the human brain, but we should
start by brushing up on the basic biology, leaning heavily on the
little book *Introducing Evolution* by Dylan Evans and Howard
Selina.

The biological basics

The theory of evolution holds that species can change, with one species giving rise to another. All life on Earth—flora or fauna—is descended from a single ancestor that lived about 4 billion years ago, and all living things carry a record of their descent in their genes. But it's the theory of 'natural selection' that explains how and why evolution happened. It provides a mechanism by which things can change their design without any outside intervention. So it's really the theory of evolution *by natural selection* we're interested in.

Natural selection occurs whenever there's a population of things that reproduce (make copies of themselves), when the copying process is less than perfect, and when the copying errors (mutations) lead to differences in the ability of offspring to survive and make copies of themselves. A mutation gives rise to a new gene not possessed by either parent.

Mutations occur randomly and can be beneficial, neutral or harmful in their effect on the organism's ability to survive and reproduce. The process of natural selection eliminates harmful mutations while passing the rarer favourable mutations on to the next generation. It's precisely because a particular mutation is beneficial to survival and reproduction that it gets passed on. Those organisms possessing the mutation will live longer or in some other way be able to produce more offspring, or offspring fitter to meet environmental challenges. Those organisms with harmful mutations won't live as long or won't have as many offspring. As the generations pass, those with beneficial mutations come to predominate and eventually the whole species changes in a way that improves its ability to reproduce itself.

These changes are 'adaptive'—they help the species solve a

problem in its environment more successfully. Over many generations, cumulative natural selection can produce complex designs such as eyes or hearts. Some feature can evolve for one purpose and then acquire another purpose. But natural selection is completely mechanical; it has no foresight. It makes a species fitter to survive and multiply in spite of the challenges the species faces, but it has no intention to do so.

'Survival of the fittest' means the fittest to reproduce. The outcome is the survival of the species; the survival of the individual is relevant only for the period in which it is still able to reproduce. But survival of the fittest shouldn't be taken to imply that organisms are continually at war with each other. Those best at co-operation may be the ones fittest to survive.

Similarly, Richard Dawkins' metaphor of the 'selfish gene' is a tricky one. Genes don't have brains, of course, but we can think of them as striving only to make more copies of themselves. This doesn't mean, however, that all animals are completely self-centred in their behaviour towards others. Biological altruism—that is, one organism doing something that helps another organism at a cost to itself—is common in nature. Many social animals give warning cries when they see a predator. This helps their fellows to get away, although it may attract the predator's attention to the one giving the cry. Another example is parents caring for their offspring.

Biological altruism focuses on effects, not motives. 'A gene which makes its bearer behave altruistically can spread through the population so long as the altruism is directed specifically at other organisms who have the same gene,' Dylan and Howard say. 'That way, the gene is still, in effect, being selfish.' The more closely related you are to another organism, the more likely you are to share the same genes with them. Studies of organisms with the same genes suggest that genes can influence behaviour. This doesn't say behaviour is completely determined by genes, but that genes have some effect. Primates also exhibit 'reciprocal altruism'—a willingness to assist others in the belief that the favour will later be returned.

Enter the human animal

The Earth is thought to be about 4.5 billion years old. Among the many kinds of mammal are the primates—monkeys and apes—which first appeared 35 million years ago. One species of ape was forced out of the forest in Africa about 5 million years ago and eventually learnt to walk upright. Hominids first appeared about 3 million years ago. One species of hominid, *Homo sapiens neanderthalensis*, probably left Africa about 300,000 years ago, much earlier than our ancestors.

Modern humans, *Homo sapiens sapiens*, first appeared around 100,000 years ago, making us a very recent species. Fully 98 per cent of human genes are also found in the chimpanzee, our closest relative. By the time our ancestors arrived in Europe, about 50,000 years ago, the Neanderthals had been there for some time. We drove the Neanderthals out to the edges of Europe and eventually they became extinct. The last Neanderthals probably lived in Spain about 35,000 years ago. They were very similar to us, with brains at least as big as ours, but it is not clear if they had language.

Humans acquired language sometime between 250,000 and 100,000 years ago and it enabled us to conquer the world. Language allows information to be shared much more effectively than the limited range of calls that other primates use. But language isn't just a means of communicating. It also allows us to think in new ways and, with the invention of writing, allows us to store and retrieve information. This increases the brain's computing power.

Dylan and Howard say culture is information that's transmitted from one generation to the next by learning rather than by genes. All cultures have many features in common: language, myth, dance, gesture, distinct sex roles, levels of social status, sexual regulations and greater public dominance by men. How is this similarity explained? Perhaps because some of these universals were developed when all humans lived in a single cultural group in Africa and perhaps because some spring from 'human nature'—the universal design features of the human mind. Evolutionary psychology is the study of the human mind from an evolutionary perspective, the scientific study of human nature.

The human mind has been shaped by natural selection as much as has the human body. Our brains have been likened to a house that's been renovated and extended over many years, particularly at the front, causing its size to double. The psychiatrist Paul McLean has simplified this extension process to three stages: we started with the reptilian brain (which gives us automatic responses to many things that happen to us), added the early mammalian brain (giving us emotional responses; also known as the 'limbic system'), and finally added the primate brain (giving us the ability to reason and control our emotions).

These different parts of the brain interact to determine the way we behave. In a paper on neuroeconomics—the study of how neuroscience can inform economics—the economist Colin Camerer and his colleagues say our behaviour emerges from the interplay between controlled and automatic systems on the one hand, and between cognitive (thinking) and affective (emotional) systems on the other. Controlled processes tend to involve step-by-step logic, be invoked deliberately, feel as if they require effort to produce and occur consciously. In contrast, automatic processes operate outside our conscious awareness and so don't feel like they require effort. Turning to the other distinction, cognitive processes evaluate facts whereas affective processes involve emotions such as anger, sadness and shame, as well as feelings such as hunger, pain and the sex drive.

The two-way classification system gives us a matrix with four quadrants representing the four modes of thinking. Quadrant I, controlled cognitive, is used when we're making very careful, conscious decisions, such as choosing between rival home loans. Quadrant II, controlled affective, is used by actors who imagine previous emotional experiences to make the audience believe the actors are experiencing those emotions. Quadrant III, automatic cognitive, governs the movement of your hands and feet as you drive a car, and Quadrant IV, automatic affective, makes you jump when somebody sneaks up behind you and also governs the fight-or-flight response.

The point is that only a tiny proportion of the things we do fall into Quadrant I in being conscious, deliberate choices. Quadrants III and IV are the brain's default mode. They whirr along all the time, constituting most of the electro-chemical activity in the brain and controlling an enormous range of our bodily reactions.

'The fashion in which the brain evolved is critical to under-standing human behaviour,' Colin says. 'In many domains, such as eating, drinking, sex and even drug use, human behaviour resembles that of our close mammalian relatives, which is not surprising because we share many of the neural mechanisms that are largely responsible for these behaviours.' Many of the processes that occur in these systems are affective rather than cognitive, being directly concerned with motivation.

People often regard behaviour as a search for pleasure or an escape from pain. But there is evidence from neuroscience that the motivation to take an action is not always closely tied to hedonic (pleasurable) consequences. The neuroscientist Ken Berridge argues that decision-making involves the interaction of two separate, though overlapping, systems: one responsible for pleasure and pain (the 'liking' system), and the other for motiv-ation (the 'wanting' system). Addiction, for instance, may cause us to want things we no longer like.

It's a mistake to think, as most conventional economists do, that humans should be—or could be—completely rational in their actions. Studies of people with damage to the emotional parts of their brain find they have difficulty making decisions. It's our emotions rather than our reason that motivate us to prefer one option over another. Other studies show that thinking too hard about our reasons for choosing something can block access to our emotional reaction and make it more likely we'll come to regret, for instance, buying what we did.

The frailties of human nature

Although we are capable of making careful, conscious decisions about important issues, there is conflict between the emotional and rational parts of our brain that often gives us a problem exercising self-control. We think it's up to us to decide how much to eat or when to stop shopping but, in fact, many of us find it very hard to restrain ourselves in the way we know we should. This is because the older, more primitive part of our brain tends to make instant decisions on an instinctive, emotional basis. The newer, more rational part of our brain tends to make more reasoned judgements, but to be a lot slower off the mark.

It's as though we have two selves: an unconscious self that's emotional and short-sighted, and a conscious self that's reasoning and far-sighted. We have trouble controlling ourselves in circumstances where the benefits are immediate and certain whereas the costs are longer term and uncertain. For instance, the reward from eating dessert is instant, whereas the costs of overeating are uncertain and far off in the future—being regarded as physically unattractive, becoming obese, developing diabetes, dying younger. As everyone knows who's tried to diet, give up smoking, control their drinking, save or get on top of their credit card debt, it's very hard to achieve the self-control our conscious, future selves want us to achieve. Many of us may have little trouble controlling ourselves in most of the behaviours I've listed, but I doubt there's anyone much who can claim to have themselves perfectly under control in every area.

Over the centuries many metaphors have been used to describe the trouble we have controlling our actions, but the one I like best comes from the psychologist Jonathan Haidt in his book *The Happiness Hypothesis*. 'Like a rider on the back of an elephant,' he says, 'the conscious, reasoning part of the mind has only limited control of what the elephant does.' The actions of the elephant, of course, are determined by instinct and emotion, and it's perfectly capable of taking us in directions we don't want to go. The point is that efforts to order the elephant to do what we want rarely succeed. The rider has to use their intelligence to train and cajole the elephant to go in the desired direction, seeking ways to get reason and emotion working together. Cognitive behavioural therapy, for instance, teaches the rider to train the elephant rather than try to defeat it directly.

Experiments with people who've had the two sides of their brains severed show that the reasoning part of our brain often just doesn't know why the faster, more instinctive part of our brain decided to do what it did, but is adept at thinking of plausible explanations for its behaviour. Psychologists call this process 'confabulation'—others call it ex-post rationalisation. In one experiment a man with a severed brain was shown a sign with the command 'wave', but in a way that couldn't be seen by the cognitive, language-controlling side of his brain. Asked why he'd waved, he replied: 'I saw somebody I knew and waved at him.' We all engage in 'erroneous sense-making'.

Other experiments have shown that we become aware of an intention to perform an action only *after* the initial wave of brain activity associated with that action. But the sensation of intention comes before the actual action. Thus we gain an impression of free will—I decided to act, so I acted—even though the brain activity that causes an action comes before we're aware of the intention and actually causes us to have the intention.

The sculpting of the brain

The environment that our minds evolved in was very different from our modern environment. As Leda Cosmides and John Tooby write in their internet primer on evolutionary psychology, our ancestors spent well over 99 per cent of our species' evolutionary history living in hunter–gatherer societies. 'That means that our forebears lived in small, nomadic bands of a few dozen individuals who got all of their food each day by gathering plants or by hunting animals,' they say. 'Each of our ancestors was, in effect, on a camping trip that lasted an entire lifetime . . .'

Through all that time, generation after generation, natural selection slowly sculpted the human brain, favouring circuitry that was good at solving the day-to-day problems of our hunter–gatherer ancestors—problems such as finding mates, hunting animals, gathering food plants, negotiating with friends, defending themselves against aggression, raising children and choosing a good habitat. Those whose circuits were better designed for solving these problems left more children, and we are descended from them.

Our species lived as hunter–gatherers 1000 times longer than as anything else, they say. The modern world of roads, grocery stores and factories has lasted for only an eyeblink of time when compared to our evolutionary history. The Industrial Revolution is a mere 200 years old. Agriculture first appeared on Earth only 10,000 years ago, and it wasn't until about 5000 years ago that as much as half of the human population engaged in farming rather than hunting and gathering.

'Natural selection is a slow process, and there just haven't been enough generations for it to design circuits that are well-adapted to our post-industrial life. In other words, our modern skulls house a stone-age mind,' Leda and John say. The key to understanding how the modern mind works is to realise that its circuits weren't designed to solve the day-to-day problems of a modern person. Our brains are better at solving the kinds of problems our ancestors faced on the African savannahs.

For instance, we are evolved to live in small groups of 20 to 200 individuals, very closely related genetically with a lifelong interaction within those small groups—a far cry from the huge numbers of relative strangers we live among today. This may help explain some of the problems we have living in big cities, but it may also mean that a desire to identify with our group, to be loyal to it and to confirm to its norms of behaviour, is basic to human nature.

Hunter–gatherer groups seem to have been highly egalitarian because of their small size and dependence on sharing each other's hunting and gathering luck. With everyone continually on the move, there was little scope for individuals to accumulate physical wealth. And, of course, hunting in particular required a high degree of co-operation between members of the group.

This challenges the notion that our evolution has made us highly selfish and competitive. A competitive urge exists, of course, but so does a co-operative urge and a concern for fairness.

The end of human evolution?

Anything that's genetic and widespread within our species must have been naturally selected. And all the traits we possess that cause us problems must once have brought us survival benefits. This is called the 'genome lag'—the insufficient time for our brains to have adapted in ways that make it easier for us to cope with the challenges of modern life.

It can be argued that, for humans, the process of biological evolution through natural selection has come to an end. Why? Because the practices of modern civilisation have caused natural selection to break down. We don't allow Nature to do the selecting and take the hindmost. Indeed, when we see the survival of the fittest occurring in nature—when we see it working 'red in tooth and claw'—something urges us to intervene and prevent such cruelty.

Modern societies intervene in the selection process by keeping alive—and thus on occasion allowing to reproduce— people who would otherwise be selected out by ill-health or misadventure. It's the very goal of medical science and the medical profession to keep the otherwise 'unfit' alive. We go to great lengths to keep 'unfit' babies alive, for instance.

In our earlier lives as hunter–gatherers it was necessary to stay alive so as to reproduce your genes. And the early deaths of those who lacked the means to stay alive caused us to be descended from those who had such ability. Staying alive required not only the ability to escape from being eaten by wild animals, to stay always alert to danger, to be cautious in tasting an unfamiliar berry that could be poisonous, and to avoid being cast out from the group, but also the ability to acquire enough food to keep body and soul together.

But a central goal of modern civilisation—of the welfare state, indeed—is to keep people alive regardless of their fitness. We have welfare payments intended to allow people to buy necessities regardless of their reason for being unable to work. If they're too young to work we pay their parents a family benefit; if they're too handicapped to work we pay them a disability support pension; if they can't work because they have dependent children but no spouse to help look after them we pay the sole-parent payment; if they can't work because they can't find a job we pay them unemployment benefits. And we have national health insurance schemes such as Medicare to ensure people's lack of means doesn't prevent them getting high-quality medical care—even if their health problem is caused by their own negligent behaviour or unhealthy lifestyle.

Psychologists have found some evidence that we still unconsciously pick mates on the basis of their likely reproductive and parental fitness—their looks and, in men, their potential as breadwinners. I heard of one experiment in which a group of men were asked what physical characteristics they preferred in a woman, and were then asked to pick from a group of women the one they preferred. Most of the men *said* they preferred women with big breasts, but the women they actually picked tended to have big hips. Even so, it's not clear that the classic markers of fitness are the only factors that influence modern humans' choice of mate.

Neuroscience has discovered that our brains possess 'mirror neurons'—specialised neurons that mirror the actions of others and thus are directly involved in imitation, anticipation and empathy. In Michael Shermer's book *The Mind of the Market*, he says the famous neuroscientist V.S. Ramachandran holds that mirror neurons are one of the key steps in making humans different from all other animals, in that by being able to imitate we can override natural selection—and consequently we can modify the environment instead of the environment modifying us (by natural selection).

'In a period of global cooling, for example, natural selection will favour those animals with more effective thermoregulation features, such as a thick fur coat,' he says. 'But this can take hundreds or thousands of generations to evolve, whereas a big-brained primate with a mirror neuron network can observe a thick-furred mammal looking toasty warm in a blizzard and immediately grasp the idea of killing the animal and wearing its fur coat rather than waiting around for evolution to grow him one.'

That's the point: although humans' biological evolution may have ended because of interference from human cultural practices, what evolutionary psychologists would call cultural evolution (and economists would call technological advance) has taken over the role of helping us adapt to our environment. Richard Dawkins has coined the term 'meme' to denote the unit of cultural evolution, just as genes are the unit of biological evolution.

Apart from our ability to use tools, our ability to speak, read and write has increased the effectiveness of cultural evolution. With language we can quickly spread the fur-coat meme (along with the stone-tool meme, the fire meme, the bow-and-arrow meme, and the art, music and religion memes). It's cultural evolution that's made us so successful as a species.

Our ability to keep improving our 'technology'—which I take to include our ability to organise societies, democracies and businesses, as well as our ability to advance our scientific understanding of how the natural world works and we ourselves work—has allowed us to produce food in abundance, prolong our lives, become more fertile, separate sex from conception, and much, much more.

My conclusion from all this is that humans have it within their power to overcome the genome lag, the fact that we live in the space age with stone-age brains. The name of the game is, first, to understand the aspects of our behaviour that are a product of our evolution and, second, to find strategies to modify our behaviour—ways to guide the elephant we're riding—in directions that allow us to live psychologically wealthier lives despite all the internal and external temptations to stay in the materialist rat race.

Why we seek happiness

One way or another, everything we do is motivated by our desire to be happy. If you're working hard in pursuit of promotion and a pay rise, you're doing it because you believe the extra status and money will make you happier.

The philosopher Blaise Pascal said: 'All men seek happiness. This is without exception. Whatever different means they employ, they all tend to this end. The cause of some going to war, and of others avoiding it, is the same desire in both, attended with different views . . . This is the motive of every action of every man, even those who hang themselves.'

The Harvard psychologist Daniel Gilbert puts it another way: 'If there has ever been a group of human beings who prefer despair to delight, frustration to satisfaction and pain to pleasure, they must be very good at hiding because no one has ever seen them. People want to be happy, and all the other things they want are typically meant to be means to that end. Even when people forgo happiness in the moment—by dieting when they could be eating, or working late when they could be sleeping—they are usually doing so in order to increase its future yield.'

If *all* of us want to be happy all the time, the explanation for this has to be in the way humans have evolved as a species. The process of natural selection must have made us that way because it improved our fitness—our ability to survive and reproduce. At one level it's very simple. Why do we find sex enjoyable? Because that makes us want to do it a lot and doing so causes us to reproduce. All of our ancestors must have enjoyed sex because that's what made them our ancestors. Those humans in the past who didn't much enjoy sex didn't get to be our ancestors.

But it's not that simple. The evolutionary biologist Randolph Nesse famously remarked that natural selection doesn't give a fig for our happiness. It just wants us alive and making babies, miserably if need be. So what's going on? Well, Daniel Nettle, a British psychologist, reveals his theory of why we are so obsessed by happiness in his book *Happiness: The Science Behind Your Smile*.

The trick is that we're biologically programmed not to *be* happy but merely to *pursue* happiness. We're programmed to pursue it in ways that contribute to our biological fitness.

Whether we actually achieve it, nature doesn't much care. So in a sense it's a bit of a con. The good news, however, is that most of us do achieve a fair bit of it. Surveys unfailingly show that most people are quite happy most of the time. Evolution has programmed us to believe we'll be happier if we're physically and materially secure, if we have a mate, if we have high social status, and many other things. All these are things that, in our primitive state, would have contributed to our fitness.

The pursuit of happiness is humanity's basic motivating force, the drive that keeps us doing and striving. And evolution is a competitive process—the survival of the fittest. So it wouldn't serve the evolutionary process's purpose if, by acquiring a mate, a bit of security and a bit of social status we could attain happiness and be content. Thus we've evolved never to be completely happy (or never for long), and to quickly adapt to whatever we've managed to attain and soon be hankering after something we imagine will be better.

One of the ways this is accomplished is by us having, as we've seen, brains with separate systems for wanting and liking. Our system of desire—run by the brain chemical dopamine—motivates us to, for instance, work long hours for things like pay rises and status goods. Our system of pleasure—run by opioids—makes us feel good while we're doing some things that are good for our fitness, though the feeling doesn't last long.

While many of the things we desire will also give pleasure, Daniel says, it isn't necessary that they do. We evolved in an environment where status was highly correlated with reproductive success, and material resources were always scarce. Since our brains haven't evolved further in response to the modern environment, they still motivate us to strive for these things in the belief they'll make us happy.

In fact, empirical research tells us the things most likely to make us happy are seeing friends, sport, cultural activities, going out and visiting new places. But so powerful is our desire system that we're often so busy pursuing money and status we don't do all that much of the things that do make us happy. Research also tells us that, beyond a certain point, societies don't get happier as they get richer (a truth politicians and economists have yet to hear about), and that the more importance people place on money, the less satisfied they are with what they've got. In other words, materialism breeds dissatisfaction with material conditions.

Yet more empirical research tells us people believe they'll be happier in the future but seldom are, and they constantly overestimate the happiness they'll get from positive developments and underestimate their ability to adjust to negative developments. In economists' jargon, we're quite bad at predicting our 'utility'.

With their assumption that people are rational—careful calculators with full knowledge of the future—economists believe that, on the odd occasion we make a mistake, we quickly learn the error of our ways. If they knew any psychology, they'd know this isn't true. Many of us go on believing the pursuit of money and status will make us happy despite loads of experience that any pleasure it brings us is fleeting.

Why? Because our system of desire is so strong. Why's it so strong? Because it suits our evolution's purpose to have us go on doing the things that (used to) improve our fitness.

The good news, however, is that natural selection has also provided us with a multi-level mind, in which the relatively automatic emotion programs that often determine our behaviour can be overridden by our better educated, more reflective selves if we go about it the right way.

3

WHO IS HAPPY?

Economics was invented to make accountants look
interesting and astrologers look accurate.

— Anon

One of the many editors I've worked for at *The Sydney Morning Herald* was a chap who was always on the lookout for stories that could justify a poster outside newsagents saying, HOW YOUR SUBURB RATES. His instincts were right: almost all of us love comparing ourselves—even the suburb we live in— with others, particularly if we're confident of rating well. One way to decide how well you're doing in the happiness stakes is to compare yourself with others. But to broaden the question out a bit, what are the characteristics of happy people? And to personalise it: what do I have to be to be happy?

In the early days of scientific study of happiness by psychologists, economists and others, much effort went into answering these questions. Government statistical agencies and polling outfits such as Gallop had for many years been asking people about their happiness—their 'subjective wellbeing'. These surveys invariably show that most people are reasonably happy.

In Australia's case, the personal wellbeing component of Professor Bob Cummins's Australian Unity Wellbeing Index shows an average wellbeing score of about 75 out of 100. On the basis of all his surveys, the doyen of happiness researchers, Professor Ed Diener, says that, except for those living in dire circumstances, most people report being happy the majority of the time, but very few report being consistently elated or extremely happy, making 'slight to moderate' happiness the rule. In America, one study of 3000 adults found that, on a scale of one to ten—from extremely unhappy to extremely happy—the average score was 6.9.

But when you divide up all these respondents according to their demographic and other life circumstances and situations you do find differences. Clearly, some categories of people are happier than others, and much effort has gone into identifying these categories and attempting to explain why they're doing better. Let me summarise that research for you—although I'll save the fascinating question of how the level of people's incomes affects happiness for a chapter of its own (Chapter 4). Hint: the results may surprise you.

Gender

Men and women are different. The processes of socialisation combine with genetics to make each gender not only physically different but experience life differently. And that leaves women happier than men. Over Bob's first 13 surveys, the average score of women was 75.7 out of 100, compared with men's average of 74.2. On average, women rate higher than men in satisfaction with each area of their lives except for safety. Whether life really is less safe for women or they just feel less safe is another question.

Women generally cope with tough situations and isolation better than men, Bob says. While the wellbeing of women living alone remains in the normal range, men who live alone have a much lower score and are at a higher risk of developing depression. And men are also harder hit should they become unemployed.

Interestingly, there is little difference in happiness between young men and young women. Once people hit the 26 to 35 year age group, however, the difference emerges dramatically, with women typically recording higher wellbeing than men. From 36 years of age onwards, the difference begins to decline.

In their book *Happiness and Economics*, Bruno Frey and Alois Stutzer, both economists from the University of Zurich, confirm that women being happier than men is typical throughout the developed world. But, they say, this seems at odds with the many studies of mental disorders revealing higher rates for women than men. However, what also distinguishes women from men is that women on average experience *both* more extreme positive emotions and more extreme negative emotions.

Women have a higher tendency to report being very happy and also a somewhat higher tendency to report being very unhappy. And the difference in the intensity of feelings may explain the reported difference in happiness. This difference in intensity may in turn be the result of gender roles. 'Women are allowed and even taught to be more emotional than men, especially when it comes to intimate relationships,' they say.

But stand by for a news flash: Bob Cummins says that over his five most recent Australian surveys the happiness difference between women and men has all but disappeared. Women, it seems, have become less happy while men have become more so. As we'll see, the same trend is happening in the United States.

Age

According to our social stereotypes, the young are happy and fancy free whereas the old, being closer to the end of their lives and having had their illusions knocked out of them, aren't all that happy. If so, happiness should decline as we age. Fortunately, it isn't true. Recent research by two economists, David Blanchflower and Andrew Oswald, has found that wellbeing is 'U-shaped over the life cycle'. So while it's true the young are happier, so too are the old. This, of course, leaves the middle-aged as the least happy on average.

Bob Cummins's wellbeing index confirms that these finding hold for Australia. People aged 18 to 35 have an average score a little higher than 76 out of 100, those aged 36 to 55 average only 74 or so, while the average for those 56 to 65 recovers to almost 76. Then the score takes off, rising to 77 for those 66 to 75, and to almost 78 for those aged over 75 years. Bob says that, although satisfaction with health declines as age-related ailments set in, older people tend to be more satisfied with other areas of their lives. David Myers, author of *The Pursuit of Happiness*, adds that, with age, our highs are less high but our lows are also less low.

In his survey of the evidence, Michael Argyle, formerly a reader in social psychology at Oxford, concludes it's the greater happiness of men that explains the higher wellbeing of the old. The old tend to have lower aspirations, and the gap between their goals and their achievements is smaller. 'People are happier in retirement if it was voluntary, if they are in good health, if they have not suffered much fall in income, and if they have active interests and activities—for example, in voluntary work, leisure groups or adult education,' he says.

Well, that's great—but what of the poor old middle-aged? The two economists' study puts the minimum point of happiness at the mid-forties. But, try as they might, psychologists can't find solid evidence in support of the widespread existence of midlife crisis. Bob Cummins's partial explanations are more prosaic. He says middle-aged people who don't live with a partner are at risk of low wellbeing. Obviously, the middle-aged are at greater risk of unemployment than the aged. And there's been a recent fall in satisfaction with the environment by people aged 36 to 65. Dave Myers adds more hopefully that seven national American studies show the empty nest is generally a happy place.

Ethnicity

Bob's surveys have little to say about ethnicity and race in Australia, but Michael Argyle says that in US studies Blacks are always found to be less happy. This is generally true of ethnic minorities. It's explained mainly by their lower incomes, education and job status, but a small effect remains after these factors are controlled for. The loss of happiness is greater for those members of minorities with higher occupational status, education and income.

Bruno Frey and his colleague say a major reason for the lower subjective wellbeing of Blacks may be lower self-esteem, which in turn is likely to be caused by their lower status in society. However, Blacks have experienced a rising trend in reported wellbeing. 'In this case, reduced discrimination has had the expected result,' they say.

Marriage

In Michael Argyle's survey of all the life circumstances affecting wellbeing he concludes that marriage is 'one of the strongest correlates of happiness'. The positive effect of marriage is still found after controlling for age, gender, income and other factors. Marriage does a little more for the happiness of women, although it does more for the physical and mental health of men.

Marriage increases happiness because it's the greatest source of social support for most people—more than friends or relations—including emotional and material support and companionship. Your spouse is involved in and often instrumental to a wide range of other satisfactions, including sex and leisure. Being in love is the greatest source of positive emotions. Marriage is good for health partly because it results in better health behaviour—married people drink and smoke less, have a better diet and do what the doctor orders. Marriage is a kind of biological co-operative whose members look after one another and receive mental health benefits, too, as a result of being able to confide in and discuss problems with a sympathetic listener. Women are better at such listening than men, which explains why men benefit more from marriage in terms of having lower rates of depression.

The significance of marriage is borne out by Bob Cummins's surveys for the Australian Unity Index. He finds that people who are married have the highest wellbeing of all marital-status groups. The average happiness of people who are married exceeds 77 out of 100. From there it is downhill all the way: people in de facto relationships average 75, well ahead of the never married on 71 or so, the separated on just under 69 and the divorced on 68. Compared with all those, the male and female widowed seem to be doing well on more than 76. But, as we'll see, this needs careful interpretation.

Bob notes that the commitment, security and support that come with a spouse help to protect wellbeing. The advantage of the legally married over de facto couples isn't as great as it appears. De facto couples tend to be younger and thus less advanced with their careers, leaving them with lower incomes. And if the de facto couple owns a home together their difference with married home-owners disappears. The symbolism and security of this commitment appears important to the de facto couple's relationship.

People who have never married tend to be younger, so their lower happiness score is partly accounted for by their lower incomes. You don't need a partner to be happy, although having one does give you an advantage in the happiness stakes. And while people with a partner have higher wellbeing on average, this is really only the case if the relationship is a happy one. Asking about the level of support people received from their partner revealed that people not receiving enough support had lower wellbeing than people living on their own.

The greater happiness of the married over those who are single, divorced or widowed persists even in cultures as diverse as those of Belarus and Spain. In their book *Happiness*, Ed Diener and his son say people's life satisfaction spikes for a period of about two years when they get married, before settling back. But when a spouse dies the widowed experience a steep decline in satisfaction, which takes about five or six years to return to close to the level it was when the spouse was still alive. This does much to explain the relatively high level of happiness among Australian widows found in Bob's survey.

Most of his respondents are likely to be old—with their spouse having died some years earlier—and to have the greater security of owning their homes.

If you're discomforted by the finding that the leap in happiness upon marriage tends not to last very long, remember that with all these results we're dealing with averages. And with every average there'll be some people above it and some below. So those couples who stay deeply in love throughout their married lives are likely to account for the above-average marriages, whereas those for whom the joy soon wears off are likely to be below average. For most people, however, passionate love is eventually replaced by companionate love.

Children

Most of the search for the 'correlates of happiness' reaches conclusions that fit nicely with our preconceived notions about the way the world should work. The married tend to be happier and so do the healthy. But there is one finding that doesn't fit the Hallmark greeting card view of wellbeing: on average, having children doesn't add to happiness. This finding is so counterintuitive that many happiness books either ignore it or play it down—'most happiness studies have not shown children to be an important cause of happiness'.

All that changed, however, when Daniel Gilbert—author of the best-selling *Stumbling on Happiness,* who even so doesn't seem a great believer in the subject—decided to reveal the profession's dirty nappy. He looked at several studies and concluded that marital satisfaction decreases dramatically after the birth of the first child and increases only when the last child has left home. He also quotes daily happiness tracking studies that show women are happier grocery shopping, eating, exercising or watching television than taking care of their kids.

This theme has been taken up with enthusiasm by Arthur Brooks, a professor of government policy at Syracuse University and author of *Gross National Happiness*. 'There are many things in a parent's life that bring great joy,' he says. 'For example, spending time away from children.'

According to a recent study by an American sociologist, parents experience lower levels of emotional wellbeing, less frequent positive emotions and more frequent negative emotions than their childless peers. The Dieners say marital satisfaction dips at the birth of the first child and continues to move down, hitting a low when kids are teenagers. When finally the kids leave home, marital satisfaction heads back up.

According to Dan Gilbert, US and European studies show that people's happiness spikes when they're *expecting* a baby, but plummets sharply after the first child is born. None of this should surprise us, he says. Every parent knows that children are a lot of work—a lot of really *hard* work—and although parenting has many rewarding moments, the vast majority of its moments involve dull and selfless service to people who will take decades to become even begrudgingly grateful for what we are doing.

But how could our cultural beliefs about the joy of parenthood be so at variance with our actual feelings? Using a cultural evolution argument, Dan says it's an example of the 'beliefs-transmission game'. If a particular belief has some property that facilitates its transmission to the next generation, then that belief tends to be held by an increasing number of minds. Generally, the accuracy of a belief is likely to increase its transmission. But inaccurate beliefs can spread if they somehow facilitate their own means of transmission. Here the means of transmitting beliefs isn't sex, as with natural selection, but communication—talking.

False beliefs that happen to promote stable societies tend to propagate because people who hold these beliefs tend to live in stable societies, which provide the means by which false beliefs propagate. The belief-transmission network of which we are a part cannot operate without a continuously replenished supply of people to do the transmitting, thus the belief that children are a source of happiness becomes a part of our cultural wisdom simply because the opposite belief unravels the fabric of any society that holds it.

Health

Everyone knows that if you've got your health you've got your happiness. And it's true—though the effect is probably not as strong as many people would expect. Sonja Lyubomirsky and colleagues find in a survey of studies that healthy people, especially older ones, declare themselves to be slightly happier than sick people. Dave Myers says more than 100 studies confirm that for adults of all ages one predictor of happiness is health and physical fitness. Ill-health—chronic pain, depleted energy or the threat of death—can undermine wellbeing.

Michael Argyle says a meta-analysis (a study of studies) found a reasonably strong overall correlation between health and happiness. This is stronger for women, and stronger when subjective rather than objective measures of health are used. He says health affects happiness partly because those in good health simply feel subjectively better, partly because they are able to do more of the things they want to do and partly because they are more socially and physically active.

Bob Cummins doesn't deny that good health adds to happiness, but he questions the converse: that poor health must cause people to be unhappy. 'Provided people have enough emotional support and financial resources to pay for treatment and medical expenses, people with poor health can be happy and experience high life quality,' he argues.

Using figures from the Australian Unity Index, he says medical conditions such as blood pressure have little effect on wellbeing. However, conditions that involve stress or pain—cancer, arthritis or diabetes—reduce wellbeing below the normal range. And illnesses such as anxiety or depression take wellbeing to very low levels.

Younger people don't cope as well with pain as older people do. While the relationship between pain and wellbeing is much the same for men and women in the younger age groups, once people reach 66 years of age women report more pain than men.

Apart from the increased health risks, people who are obese are subjected to a certain amount of discrimination for their condition. It's thus not surprising that happiness also suffers once people reach a moderate or severe level of obesity. However, most people whose weight falls within the mild obesity range manage to maintain normal levels of wellbeing. Married people who are obese have lower wellbeing than married people in the healthy weight range. Yet obesity doesn't seem to affect married people as drastically as those who aren't married.

Education

Many surveys have found a correlation between educational level and happiness, according to Michael Argyle, but the effect is small. The effect of education is strongest in the developing countries and weakest in the United States, where it's been declining over time. Education is closely linked to income and occupational status and, indeed, can be a precursor of both. A meta-analysis found that education contributed to wellbeing primarily by affecting occupation rather than income, and that it had a rather small effect apart from this.

The education effect on happiness is strongest for people with low incomes. Any additional effect education has, apart from its effect on occupation and income, may be due to the social status conveyed by the education. This could explain the stronger effect in developing countries. In developed countries education's pure contribution to the happiness of those with low incomes is by creating wider interests, especially leisure interests.

Employment

Bob Cummins's Australian Unity surveys show that the average wellbeing of Australians with full-time jobs is a fraction higher that the overall average. Other studies show that the self-employed are happier than employees, presumably because they enjoy being their own boss.

But the strongest proof of the contribution employment makes to wellbeing is its absence: the unemployed are particularly unhappy. According to Bob's findings the happiness of the unemployed averages 66.5, compared with the full-time employed's 75.5. The scores for the unemployed are significantly worse for men than for women, probably because the wellbeing of men is more heavily dependent on their work status.

Unemployed men are thus a high-risk group for depression, with Australia's suicide rate being four times higher for men than women. The devastating impact of unemployment is seen when it's combined with another factor, such as separation or divorce, which makes the risk of depression even higher.

All this raises the issue of whether unemployment is voluntary; whether people choose to be unemployed—because unemployment benefits are too generous and because working is . . . well, too much like hard work. In the Australian context, it goes to the allegation of dole bludging. You don't hear many people talking that way in recent times, but I've been around long enough to know that concerns about dole bludging are cyclical. They disappear during recessions (when you and I are worried about losing our own jobs), but re-emerge when the recession is a fading memory and it's easy to convince ourselves that anyone who really wants a job could get one.

In a British study by two economists, Andrew Clark and Andrew Oswald, they measured unhappiness rather than happiness, using Britain's general health questionnaire. This produces a measure of mental stress running from zero to 12, with zero representing perfectly happy and 12 something too awful to contemplate. Long before you hit 12 you're classed as someone who 'would benefit from psychiatric treatment'.

Clark and Oswald find that the unemployed are twice as unhappy as the employed. The *average* distress score of 1.5 jumps to three in the case of the jobless. Being unemployed is enough to change a particular *individual's* distress level from zero to two, or from one to four, or from four to eight. In other words, the unhappier you are before becoming unemployed, the worse the effect of becoming unemployed is likely to be.

What's more, the researchers found that joblessness depresses wellbeing more than any other single characteristic, including divorce or separation.

But now we come to the tricky bit. Though it's clear the unemployed as a class are much more unhappy than people with jobs, among the unemployed there are different degrees of unhappiness. For instance, there's been a lot of community concern about the very high rate of youth unemployment. Some people believe it's worse for young people to be unemployed than for adults. But the study finds that, in terms of mental distress, the young suffer least from the absence of a job. The age group that suffers most is people aged between 30 and 49.

There's been concern about the concentration of unemployment in certain depressed areas—Wollongong, for instance. But the study finds that unemployed people who live in regions of high unemployment don't feel quite so bad about it as do unemployed who live in regions of low unemployment. This finding fits with other research which found that attempted suicide by unemployed men (relative to employed men) in Edinburgh is less common in high-unemployment parts of the city.

Unemployment is more prevalent among the less-skilled, who you'd expect to have less savings (and possibly less access to networks of support) than the better-paid. But the study finds that distress from joblessness is, at 3.4, greatest for those who are highly educated.

Many economists believe that the greatest concern about unemployment should be focused on the long-term unemployed—those who've been jobless for a year or more. Indeed, I've been known to make the fearless statement that I'm not worried about unemployment, only about long-term unemployment. But the study finds that distress is greatest among those who have recently lost their job. As the duration of unemployment lengthens, the degree of distress declines.

I suppose that, when you think about it, there is a certain human logic to these initially surprising findings. One thing they seem to be saying is that, for humans, there's comfort in numbers, that people don't like being the odd one out. This may explain why individuals who live in areas where they're surrounded by unemployment don't feel quite so bad about their own unemployment. It may also explain why young people don't feel as bad about being unemployed, knowing that unemployment is much higher among the young. Perhaps there's less stigma attached to being unemployed in these circumstances. It may even help explain why the higher-educated feel worse about being unemployed—unemployment is much less common among the higher-educated.

As for the finding that the long-term unemployed are less unhappy than the recently unemployed, I see it as evidence of the indomitability of the human spirit. No matter how bad things are, we can get used to anything.

It's important to appreciate that the unhappiness the jobless feel is greater than can be accounted for by the loss of income involved. So there seems also to be an effect on self-esteem, as is shown by the fact that the retired—who also don't work—are generally happy. Michael Argyle says there's probably also an effect from commitment to work, particularly among older white men. These findings show the partly hidden benefits of work in, for example, structuring time and providing social life and self-image.

Religion

Religiously committed people are more likely to rate themselves as very happy. This is a widely found phenomenon in wellbeing surveys in other countries. Bob Cummins's survey results for Australia, however, put it in a different light. His respondents are asked how they feel about their spiritual fulfilment or religion. The 12 per cent who say they don't have this in their lives report normal levels of wellbeing, whereas among those who say they do have spiritual or religious experience, their happiness scores don't get up into the normal range until their self-nominated strength of that experience reaches seven or more on a scale of zero to ten. But those nominating eight have happiness scores that are above average, while those saying nine are well above average and those saying ten hit a score of almost 81 out of 100.

How are we to interpret these results? I think the fact that a mere 12 per cent of respondents professed no spiritual or religious experience suggests a problem with the open-endedness of the question. Since the proportion of the Australian population attending Christian churches each week is less than 10 per cent, it's likely that many respondents interpreted the reference to 'spiritual experience' very broadly and then expressed only a very weak strength of experience. If those respondents with a more formal commitment to religion tended to nominate very strong degrees of such experience this would put their wellbeing score in the same above-average range as has been found in overseas surveys of religious commitment.

In Bruno Frey's summary of the overseas evidence he notes that the positive correlation between believing in God and happiness holds even after controlling for marital status, income and age. He proposes several reasons why religion raises happiness. Church attendance is an important source of social support. Particularly for people who have lost other kinds of support—such as older people and widows—religious activities and the sense of communion experienced provide an effective substitute.

Religion offers an 'interpretative framework' that can instil life with meaning and purpose. The feeling of being close to God and the belief in an afterlife provide existential certainty and are thus a source of happiness. Religious people are better able to cope with adverse circumstances since a bad event can be better overcome when it is attributed to the will of God. Finally, church members are on average of better health, mainly because they drink and smoke less and are sexually less promiscuous, and they therefore live longer.

Beauty

There's a load of evidence from psychology that good-looking people enjoy many advantages over those of plain appearance. They are, for instance, more likely to be hired, and more likely to be promoted and paid more highly. So that makes it all the more surprising that, on average, the good-looking aren't any happier than the rest of us. Indeed, one study even found that fashion models are significantly *less* happy than their peers, possibly because they are more likely to be judged for their looks alone and have fewer opportunities to develop meaningful relationships or exert personal control within their jobs.

More to our purpose, a study by Ed Diener and some colleagues found that, whereas the happiest participants tended to believe they were attractive, objective judges (who examined photos or videos of people they didn't know) didn't regard them as any nicer looking than their less happy peers.

But here's a question: if *you* think you're good-looking, what does it matter what others think? Sonja Lyubomirsky says there's evidence that happy people are somewhat more likely to perceive *everything* about their lives, including their appearance, in more positive, optimistic ways. So becoming objectively more beautiful—by means of cosmetic surgery, for example—is unlikely to make most people happier. But coming to believe you're beautiful is another matter because research suggests this may be one of many happiness boosters.

Country living

In a special survey he carried out in 2005, Bob Cummins examined Australians' reported wellbeing according to where they live. It turns out that people who live in country towns enjoy higher levels of personal wellbeing than those who live in Australia's eight capital cities. They tend to score higher on satisfaction with personal achievements, personal relationships, personal safety and feelings of connectedness with the community.

Whoever said there's safety in numbers wasn't thinking about life in big cities. The respondents from capital cities had less satisfaction with safety and community connection than people living in all other locations. There's a significant contradiction here: living cheek by jowl with many people makes you feel less connected to your community, not more. Large cities are more impersonal. But a high degree of community connection—'social capital' as it's sometimes called—engenders a greater sense of personal safety.

One qualification to the pattern of country people feeling more satisfied than city people is that people in *remote* areas are no happier than cityslickers. They're a lot less satisfied with the economic situation, with business and with government. This may reflect the long-running difficulties in rural industry. Women are more satisfied than men in every location, but the difference is greatest in remote locations.

Among adults, the higher personal wellbeing in country towns is limited to those in the 26 to 55 years age group. This is the age range when people are most likely to be living with children—which may affect perceptions of community connectedness and safety.

But it would be wrong to conclude that life is equally dismal in each of the capital cities. Some are worse than others. Of the eight, the two their denizens rate worst are Sydney and Perth. Huh? Well, Sydney's lower sense of personal wellbeing is easily accounted for—it's the city with by far the highest population (4 million) and population density (1900 people per square kilometre). But that doesn't account for Perth. Its population is neither particularly big nor tightly packed—about the same as Brisbane, in fact. It may be a sense of isolation. Bob says Perth is one of the most isolated cities on Earth, and the locals may feel that the action (not to mention a lot of the state's mineral wealth) is 'back east'. The two most satisfied cities—because of their higher scores on national as opposed to personal wellbeing issues—are Brisbane and Melbourne. Both have high levels of satisfaction with government, the natural environment and national security.

Be that as it may, one possibility Bob didn't consider is that city people are less satisfied because of all the time they spend feeling guilty about their country cousins. And to think our sympathy is wasted.

Nations

Talk about how your suburb rates . . . There are a couple of outfits that regularly produce league tables of which nations are happiest and—surprise, surprise—such rankings get a lot of publicity in the media. Trouble is, the rival tables don't agree on who's best. At one point, in 2006, the World Map of Happiness, compiled by an academic at the University of Leicester, nominated Denmark and various other European countries as happiest, whereas the Happy Planet Index, compiled by the New Economics Foundation in association with Friends of the Earth, nominated Vanuatu and various small Latin American countries as happiest.

When Daniel Ben-Ami investigated he found that neither league table measured happiness. The first seemed to combine self-reported happiness with access to schooling, life expectancy and gross domestic product per person; the second combined life satisfaction with life expectancy and divided it by each country's 'ecological footprint'. It was the inclusion of the latter measure that ousted the European countries from the top places and installed the developing countries.

In their book *Happiness*, the Dieners quote the more reliable results obtainable from the Gallup World Survey of 2006. Random samples of about 1000 people in each of 130 countries were asked to evaluate their lives overall. The top ten countries started with Denmark on eight out of ten, then Finland and the Netherlands on 7.6, then Norway and Switzerland on 7.5, followed by New Zealand, Australia, Canada, Belgium and Sweden on 7.4. The bottom ten countries included seven African countries, plus Georgia, Cambodia and Haiti.

The Dieners conclude from these results that the countries with the highest wellbeing are economically developed, democratic, high in human rights and high in equal rights for women. In contrast, the countries with the lowest life satisfaction tend to be extremely poor, are often politically unstable and experience conflict within and with neighbouring countries. 'What this demonstrates,' they say, 'is that not all happiness comes from within, as many pundits claim—to feel satisfied with one's life it is important to live in secure circumstances where one's needs can be met.'

Even after you control for a country's income, several societal characteristics are important to happiness. Longevity, for example, correlates with life satisfaction. Combining low incomes, political instability, major health concerns, government corruption and human rights problems can create a culture in which many people experience very low happiness.

Political views

I'm not sure how seriously you should take this—because it's not a finding that's been widely replicated—but there is some evidence that people with conservative political views are happier than those with progressive or, as the Americans would put it, liberal views. A study by two psychologists from New York University examined various surveys of the political attitudes of Americans and the citizens of eight other Western countries. It found that conservatives are happy but liberals are angry—even after controlling for differences in income, education and religion.

The authors suggest the explanation lies in the way people from the two sides rationalise inequality. In the case of the surge in home foreclosures prompted by America's sub-prime lending crisis, for instance, a conservative might explain it simply in terms of the borrowers' poor economic choices, whereas a liberal might seethe over predatory lenders and lax government regulation.

In his examination of 2004 survey data, Arthur Brooks of Syracuse University found that Americans who called themselves conservative or very conservative were nearly twice as likely to tell pollsters they were very happy as those who considered themselves liberal or very liberal. This pattern was nothing new, having existed for at least 35 years.

He thinks several factors help to explain this finding. Conservatives are twice as likely as liberals to be married and twice as likely to attend church every week. Married, religious people are more likely than secular singles to be happy. And when you combine these two factors they become more powerful. Secular liberals are as likely to say they're not too happy as to say they're very happy, whereas religious conservatives are ten times more likely to report being very happy than not too happy.

Personality traits

So far we've dealt mainly with the socio-demographic circumstances of happy people—their gender, age, race, marital and parental status, education and employment. If instead we look at people's traits of personality, what do they tell us about who's happy? What kind of personality do I need to be happy?

In his book *The Mind of the Market*, Michael Shermer summarises nicely the four main personality traits that correlate highly with happiness. First is high self-esteem. Happy people like themselves and believe themselves to be healthier, more intelligent, more ethical, less prejudiced and better able to get along with other people.

Second, personal control. Happy people have the freedom to control their own lives, their choices and decisions, and therefore life outcomes. People lacking such freedom typically suffer lower levels of happiness, morale and even health—people such as prisoners, long-term care patients, citizens of impoverished countries and citizens of totalitarian regimes.

Third, optimism. Happy people view the world in a more positive manner, tending to see the good in others and in events. Fourth, extroversion. Happy people are personally outgoing and socially gregarious. They like being around other people, and that in turn brings them more social contacts and opportunities for warm and caring relationships.

Who isn't happy

If all those are the categories of people who tend to be happier than average, who are the poor sods a lot less happy than normal? We've mentioned some of them on the way through, but it's worth looking at the question specifically. Bob Cummins says the three factors that do most to reduce wellbeing are having a very low income (a household income of less than $15,000 a year), living alone or as a single parent and being unemployed. To that we could add mental ill-health.

The group with the lowest wellbeing discovered by Bob's Australian Unity Wellbeing surveys are carers—people who provide unpaid care and support to a family member or friend who is frail, has a disability, is mentally ill or has a chronic condition. Remembering that the overall average level of wellbeing is 75 out of 100, carers' average level is a bit over 58. Only a third of carers are depression-free and another third suffer from severe or extremely severe depression.

People suffering from anxiety have a wellbeing level averaging 63, while all those suffering from depression average 65.

The average wellbeing of the unemployed is a bit more than 66, but for those who live alone it falls to 60. Taken by itself, having an income below $15,000 isn't good, but it isn't too terrible: such people have a wellbeing level of 71. Similarly, living alone isn't too bad: such people average 72. It's when you start combining some of those circumstances—and maybe throwing in mental ill-heath—that you get really unhappy people.

Finally, spare a thought for those people renting their home—which would include some youngsters who're as happy as Larry, but many more people who are unemployed, unwell or with very low incomes and maybe all three. Overall, renters' wellbeing averages 69, compared with 74 for home-owners with mortgages and 77 for those who own their homes outright.

Is happiness a cause or an effect?

Before we move on, there's something I must make clear. So far in this chapter I've written only about the correlations between happiness and various socio-demographic characteristics. We saw, for instance, that the married tend to be happier than the unmarried. But, as I'm sure you remember from university, correlation is not causation. Does being married make you happier, or is it just that happy people are more likely to get married? That's a question mere correlation can't answer.

Initially, the happiness researchers devoted their efforts mainly to looking for correlations—and I've just summarised their findings for you. More recently, they've given greater attention to trying to establish the 'direction of causation', something they can get nearer to if, instead of just looking at 'cross-sectional' data at a point in time—how many marrieds in 2004 also said they were happy—they look at 'longitudinal' (or panel) data, in which the experiences of particular individuals are followed over a number of years.

Sometimes, however, determining causation is just a matter of logic. For instance, it's clear that our age influences our happiness because, though being of a certain age could affect how happy you were, being happy or unhappy can't affect how old you are. Similarly, since about 90 per cent of people get married at some point in their lives, it seems pretty clear that marriage leads to happiness, not vice versa.

Several studies suggest that religion causes happiness rather than happiness causing people to be religious. One study found that whether people attended church was a good predictor of how happy they were 15 years later. Another study found that religious experiences produced enhanced happiness up to six months later. Religious conversion has similar effects: those affected are often in a state of anxiety and distress before the event, but feel at peace afterwards.

Longitudinal studies have been used to demonstrate that employment leads to wellbeing. A British study looked at steel workers before and after the closure of their works. Those who hadn't found jobs six months later had much lower scores on a test of positive feelings than those who had. Another study looked at 2000 young people in Leeds before they left school and at two-yearly intervals afterwards. Those who didn't find jobs became less mentally well over the next one and two years, whereas those who did find jobs became better.

But perhaps the most effort has been put into examining the causal links between health and happiness. Are people happy because they're healthy, or are people healthier because they're happy? Researchers are now quite confident of the answer to that: both. Yes, healthy people are happier, but yes, being happier makes you healthier.

The Dieners say, 'ample evidence now indicates that happiness is very important to your health'. Sonja Lyubomirsky and her colleagues say happy people are more likely to show greater self-control and self-regulatory and coping abilities, to have a bolstered immune system and even to live a longer life (which slightly qualifies my earlier assertion that happiness can't affect your age).

So becoming happier doesn't just make you *feel* good, it brings with it a lot of fringe benefits. And better health is just the start of those benefits. Sonja's survey of evidence finds that, compared with their less happy peers, happier people are more sociable and energetic, more charitable and co-operative and better liked by others. Happier people are more likely to get married and stay married, and to have richer networks of friends and social support.

They show more flexibility and ingenuity in their thinking, and are more productive in their jobs. They are better leaders and negotiators, and earn more money. Which brings us to an important question: are people happy because they're successful or are they successful because they're happy? Both. The first half is easy to believe, but now researchers have amassed evidence to support the second half. Sonja, Ed Diener and a colleague reviewed 225 studies and concluded that happiness breeds success. Happy individuals are predisposed to seek out and undertake new goals in life, which often brings them even more happiness.

The bad news

So, there you have it. If you want to be happier, all you have to do is turn yourself into an older, white, religious, healthy, rural, conservative, employed married woman with grown-up kids. While you're at it, make sure you're an optimistic extrovert, big on personal control and self-esteem. Do this and you'll not only be happy but also successful, which will make you happier still. But you don't have to be good-looking.

Hardly useful advice? No, it isn't. The trouble with all those socio-demographic circumstances is that many of them can't be changed—your gender, age and race—while most of the others can be changed only with great difficulty or disruption: marital status, children, religious and political inclinations, city address, education and health. Even ceasing to be unemployed would be a tall order for many people. As for the desirable character traits, they tend to be things we inherit from our parents (although, as we'll see in Chapter 6, they can be modified with effort).

A point to note is that even if you're fortunate enough to find yourself on the right side of those socio-demographic circumstances—you're a white, non-middle-aged married woman, and so on—each individual item doesn't push your happiness much higher than the overall average. It's not a huge advantage to be a woman, to be married, to have a high income, to have religious faith.

Why not? Because of the great human quality the psychologists call 'hedonic adaptation'. Because our aspirations and expectations adjust. Because we so quickly get used to a higher income, being married, having a good education. Some famous studies have found that people who win the lottery don't take long to return to their former degree of happiness, while people suffering serious setbacks often approach their earlier level of life satisfaction after a few years. (Research finds two situations where adaptation is particularly weak: it takes about seven years for widows to regain their previous happiness level, and the effects of losing your job can linger long after you've gained another one.)

A second reason the happiness advantage from the possession of some socio-demographic characteristics is small is that it can diminish over time. Very recent research by a young Australian economist at the University of Pennsylvania's Wharton School, Justin Wolfers, and his colleague Betsey Stevenson has found that, although the inequality of people's incomes has widened in the United States over the past 30 years, the inequality in people's self-assessed happiness has narrowed over the same period. Examining the answers people have given to the happiness question in America's regular General Social Survey since 1972, Justin and Betsey found that the proportion of the population choosing the middle category of 'pretty happy' rose from 52 per cent in the 1970s to 56 per cent in the most recent decade. This change is the combined effect of fewer people saying they're 'very happy' and fewer saying they're 'not too happy'.

That's an interesting finding, but of greater relevance to our present purpose are the pair's findings that the past 30 years have seen the gap between women's and men's happiness scores disappear, and the gap between whites' and blacks' happiness scores decline by two thirds. At the same time, however, the gap between highly and lowly educated people's happiness scores has widened substantially.

The good news

But if the bad news is that there's not a lot you can do to increase your happiness by changing your socio-demographic circumstances, the good news is that those circumstances don't account for a lot of your overall happiness. As we saw in Chapter I, the happiness experts believe the factors that influence the level of a person's happiness fall into three categories: their inherited set range, their life circumstances and their voluntary, intentional activity.

Recent research by Sonja Lyubomirsky and colleagues supports the 'stylised facts' that a person's set-point accounts for about 50 per cent of the difference in their happiness level and the circumstances of their life account for about 10 per cent, leaving factors under their voluntary control—and thus able to be influenced by their intentional activity—accounting for as much as 40 per cent.

So the good news comes in two parts. The first is that the personality traits known to influence our happiness—whether we're optimists and extroverts, etcetera—being largely inherited from our parents, help to determine our 50 per cent set range. The second is that all the socio-demographic circumstances of our lives—to which I devoted this chapter—combine to determine only about 10 per cent of the difference between our level of happiness and those of other people. That's good news because it's so difficult—and in some cases impossible—for us to change those circumstances.

I started this chapter with the question: what do I have to be to be happy? And I answered it. You have to be female, white, not middle-aged, married, and so forth. It's an interesting question, but it yields a frustrating answer because it's so difficult to *be* something you're not. In other words, it's the wrong question. Becoming happier is not about *being* something different, it's about *doing* something different. And that's good news because it *is* possible for us to change the way we behave—with enough effort.

The Dieners conclude that happiness is more than achieving desirable life circumstances such as health, wealth, success at work and a happy family. Happiness is much more a process than an emotional destination. It's not so much about acquiring a list of desirable circumstances—a good house in a good suburb, a well-paid, high-status job, a considerate spouse—as it is about learning to live our lives in a positive, happy way.

But don't forget this, a much more recent insight from the science of happiness: finding ways to become happier doesn't just make you feel better, it's also good for you in a number of ways. It brings a lot of fringe benefits. There's growing evidence that it makes you more successful—not just in earning money and status, but in our pursuit of good health and satisfying relationships.

So if becoming happier is about doing rather than being, just what do you have to do? That's the question I'll try to answer in Chapter 6.

4

MONEY AND HAPPINESS

What good is happiness? It can't buy money.
— Henny Youngman

Many people, perhaps most, profess to believe that money can't buy happiness. Certainly, few are willing to directly contradict that virtuous sentiment. (Those with doubts usually say something like, 'I've been rich and I've been poor, and I know which I prefer.') But although we pay lip service, our actions suggest we regard money and the things it buys as very important.

So I guess it's no surprise that the question, Does money buy happiness?, is one of never-ending interest to most of us. In the years leading up to the writing of this book I've had a daily Google search on the word 'happiness' and I've lost count of the number of times some newspaper somewhere in the world has run a story about the latest twist or turn in the happiness research with a headline saying, No it Doesn't—or, in roughly equal measure, Yes it Does.

Well, what's it to be? To most economists it's a no-brainer: of course money buys happiness—why do you think we do what we do all day? But, in truth, the answer from the happiness researchers is not that simple—as our undiminished interest in the old question implies. What's more, the answer keeps getting less simple as more evidence comes to hand. Happiness is a young science.

Yes it does . . .

So what do the psychologists and economists who specialise in the subject say: does money buy happiness? Yes it does—up to a point. Beyond that point, it's not value for money, so to speak. I guess I should explain.

If you take a developed country such as Australia and divide everyone according to the size of their household income, you find that the higher their income the happier they report being. For his Australian Unity Wellbeing Index Bob Cummins, a psychology professor at Deakin University, divides respondents into eight income categories. Remembering that the overall average happiness score is 75 out of 100, those respondents in the lowest category, receiving less than $15,000 a year, had an average score of 71.3. Those receiving $15,000 to $30,000 averaged 73.4, those on $31,000 to $60,000 averaged 74.7, those on $61,000 to $100,000 averaged 76.2 and those on $101,000 to $150,000 averaged 77.7.

That would account for the great majority of respondents (remember that many would come from two-income households), but let's keep going: those on $151,000 to $250,000 had an average happiness score of 79.1, those on $251,000 to $500,000 averaged 79.5 and those earning more than $500,000 a year averaged 81.1. So there you are: dividing people up according to their incomes gives average happiness scores that climb from 71.3 at the bottom to 81.1 at the top. Such a gradient is typical of the developed countries and is the main reason for saying, yes, there is a clear correlation between money and happiness.

But as long ago as 1974, Richard Easterlin, an economic historian now at the University of Southern California, discovered a paradox: if you took the countries of the world—or, at least, those few for which figures on happiness were available—you found the relationship between income and wellbeing was patchy. There was quite a strong correlation for the poor countries, but once average income per person exceeded about US$15,000 a year it became quite weak. Among the developed countries, levels of both income and happiness were higher, but those nations with the greatest happiness weren't necessarily those with the highest incomes.

In the case of the United States, although its income per person had doubled since the early post-war period, its average level of happiness hadn't changed. Other researchers discovered that much the same was true for Japan and various European countries.

Although at any point in time in a particular country higher income-earners are happier than lower income-earners, once the people of that country have reached a basic standard of living further increases in the country's level of income will do little or nothing to increase its average level of happiness. From that point on, *absolute* economy-wide increases in income won't raise average wellbeing because the only thing that makes people happier is an increase in their *relative* income (and, obviously, any increase in some people's relative income would be offset by a decline in other people's relative income).

. . . up to a point

Although some disagreement with all this has emerged in recent years, it's important to note that few have challenged an important element of the conventional wisdom among happiness researchers: the presence of 'diminishing marginal utility'. In other words, as your income rises it gets harder and harder to achieve an increase in your happiness. DMU is an economists' concept, which I always explain by saying that your third ice cream never tastes as good as your first. And your fourth does even less for you than your third.

DMU is evident from Bob Cummins's figuring. Using those figures from the Australian Unity Wellbeing Index for happiness by income that I've already quoted, Bob has calculated the cost of purchasing an extra percentage point of wellbeing. Let's say you have an income of less than $15,000 (say, because you were on the single pension) and your happiness level is 71. According to these averages, a rise in your income of just over $7000 a year would raise your happiness to 72.

But now the rot sets in. For someone in the $15,000 to $30,000 income bracket to enjoy a 1 percentage point increase in their happiness would 'cost' $23,000 a year. In the next bracket, $31,000 to $60,000, the cost rises to $26,000. In the $61,000 to $100,000 bracket the cost rises by a quarter to more than $33,000. In the $101,000 to $150,000 bracket it more than doubles to $71,000. And for the $151,000 to $250,000 income bracket the cost of an extra 1 percentage point of happiness rises by a factor of more than eight to $625,000 a year. No, it's not a misprint.

That is where Bob stops his calculations, but let's take it one notch further. Say you're the highly ambitious type and, by getting a huge promotion or by greatly improving the business you own, you could raise your household's income from the $251,000 to $500,000 a year bracket to something over $500,000. If you're typical of the people already in that position you'd raise your happiness level by just 0.6 percentage points.

Why money buys so little extra happiness

Now *that's* diminishing marginal utility. It leaves the relationship between money and happiness looking pretty weak for most people in the developed economies. Economists and others who believe the link between economic growth and subjective wellbeing is a no-brainer—that is, I've never bothered to think about it—have a case to answer: why does increased income yield so little value for money to those who want to buy more happiness?

The psychologists long ago developed a metaphor that individuals in developed countries are on a kind of 'hedonic treadmill'—we keep trying to move forward by earning more and spending more, but this never does much to make us happier. Have you ever had that feeling? I have.

So why? The first part of the psychologists' explanation is 'adaptation'. The ability of humans to adjust to changed conditions—whether physical or psychic—is one of our most fundamental and valuable characteristics. If you've heard of the boiling frog—the frog in the pot of water that didn't notice the gradual increase in the temperature until the water was boiling—you know about our ability. We react to noticeable changes—had the water in the pot gone straight from cool to hot, the frog would have noticed—and then quickly adjust to the changed circumstances.

This, by the way, explains why we seek out novel experiences, look forward to a change of pace or geography—I always look forward to holidays, but then look forward to getting back to work—and develop new goals once old ones have been met. So the trouble with promotions and pay rises, and with all the new things we can buy with the extra money that comes our way, is that the pleasure we feel soon wears off. We quickly become habituated to our newly improved circumstances and come to regard them as part of the status quo.

To demonstrate the power of adaptation to keep us from getting further on the hedonic treadmill, psychologists often quote a famous study showing that people who'd won the lottery soon went back to feeling no happier than they were before. It's true that winning a huge sum can sometimes disrupt a winner's life in ways that make them unhappy: they lose friends—either because they refuse requests for help or because their friends don't want others to think they're sucking up—or they move to a flash house in a flash suburb and find the neighbours don't want to know them. But such well-told stories aren't necessarily typical. In any case, in their book *Happiness* Ed Diener and his son Robert Biswas-Diener spoil the fun by advising that other more intensive studies of lottery winners found them to be happier than other people, with this effect persisting over time.

However, Ed also asked the Princeton psychologist Daniel Kahneman, who won the Nobel Prize in *economics* for his pioneering work in behavioural economics and happiness, how long the emotional glow lasted. Winning the Nobel is a big deal, of course, bringing huge media attention, attractive offers of book contracts and honorary doctoral degrees. Daniel said it was good fun for about a year, primarily because of all the social invitations, but then it was back to business as usual.

Ed just happened to be collecting daily happiness figures from a 21-year-old student he calls Henry during the 80 days in which Henry was being treated for Hodgkin's disease. Henry received news that the treatment had been effective in wiping out his cancer, putting him into full remission. Henry's moods fluctuated daily, sometimes bouncing into joyous feelings and sometimes spilling into the blues. When, halfway through the study, Henry received the good news, his happiness leapt. But the euphoria of beating cancer lasted only a day or two and he returned to a level of happiness just a bit higher than his previous average. That's the power of adaptation.

The good thing about our adaptability is that it works in both directions—we're just as good at getting used to the setbacks and other disappointments that come our way. That's why you'll never find a psychologist bewailing the existence of adaptation. It's the mechanism that brings about the indomitability of the human spirit—though the oft-quoted study purporting to find that people made paraplegics by accidents soon return to their former happiness has been misrepresented. There *are* limits to adaptation.

But while the psychologists may spruik the benefits of our inbuilt adaption mechanism, you and I may wonder what's so wonderful about our ability to lose the appreciation of our good fortune so quickly. The Dieners have the answer: 'Returning to our mildly pleasant baseline allows us the room to experience the emotional highs and euphoria of exceptional events when they come along. If we did not have some room for growth in happiness, we would not care about personal growth, new goals or exciting surprises.' Get it? As we discussed in Chapter 2, adaptation is part of the evolutionary mechanism designed to keep us busy.

Aspiration and social comparison

Adaptation says we get nowhere on the hedonic treadmill because we so quickly come to take for granted the advances we've made. An alternative possibility is that we soon become dissatisfied with what we have because our aspirations adjust. You've probably heard of the opinion polls that ask people whether they're satisfied with their income or whether just 'a little more' money would make them happy. Invariably, most people say they need just a little more. And they say it year after year no matter how much their actual income has risen over the years. Indeed, when asked how much extra they need, the sum they nominate tends to increase pretty much in line with their actual incomes.

When Clive Hamilton, then director of the Australia Institute, commissioned an opinion poll in 2002, he found that 62 per cent of respondents believed they couldn't afford to buy everything they really needed. And 56 per cent said they spent nearly all their money on the basic necessities of life. It's our ever-rising aspirations that turn what were once seen as luxuries—two cars, flat screen television sets, air-conditioning in car and home, overseas holidays—into supposed necessities.

The Dieners quote the example of two couples they know where both husband and wife are university professors. One couple, whom they call the Johnsons, earn a combined income of $100,000 a year. The other, the Thompsons, earn $200,000 a year. You'd expect the Thompsons to be happier than the Johnsons. Indeed, if you hadn't heard of the diminishing marginal utility of money, you'd expect the Thompsons to be twice as happy as the Johnsons. But either conclusion is wrong because it takes no account of their aspirations. Remember the formula:

$$Happiness = \frac{What\ we\ have\ (attainments)}{What\ we\ want\ (aspirations)}$$

The Thompsons' desires are for foreign travel, luxury cars, an expensive house, the latest electronic gadgets and private schools. Unfortunately, these are worth about double the Thompsons' income, which leaves them with an (un)happiness quotient of 0.5. By contrast, the Johnsons' desires run to modest house and car, some travel, social leisure, health insurance and inexpensive lessons for their children. These are worth about half the Johnsons' income, giving them a very high happiness quotient of two.

Why, in Bob Cummins's figuring for Australia, are high-income people only a little happier than people on lower-middle incomes? Perhaps because people on modest incomes do more to keep their material aspirations in check.

The psychologists believe our aspirations are driven by what they call 'social comparison' and what I'd call our drive for status. The incomes we earn perform various functions. The most obvious is that we can use the money to buy things. But another is that we can view the amount of money we earn as an indicator of our success at playing the capitalist game and thus of our social status. So many of us have an interest in earning more that's actually independent of our interest in being able to buy more stuff.

Although most of us don't like to admit it, I believe virtually all of us are into social comparison—it's been bred into us—and most of us are keen to raise our social status or, failing that, at least keep up with the Joneses. This doesn't mean we all compare ourselves with Australia's richest man—though I bet the second-richest man does, continually—but that we choose our own relevant 'reference groups': the people in our street, in our suburb, our siblings and in-laws, our workmates, and so forth.

Of course, in many cases, though we and a few close associates know how much we earn, most of the people around us don't. Sometimes it's enough for them to know our occupation or job title but, if it's not clear to those around us just how well we're doing, all is not lost. Here's a novel suggestion: why don't you demonstrate to everyone how well you're doing by buying really expensive stuff? Oh, I guess it's not such a new idea—the American economist Thorstein Veblen was writing about what he dubbed 'conspicuous consumption' more than 100 years ago.

We demonstrate to the world how well we're doing by the suburb and house we live in, the car we drive, the clothes we wear and dress our kids in, the schools we send our children to, and much else. In the 1970s another economist, Fred Hirsch, introduced the concept of 'positional goods'—goods (or services) that, as well as doing whatever it is they're supposed to do, also demonstrate the high position we occupy in the pecking order. If, for instance, a perfectly comfortable, safe and efficient Toyota could get us from A to B at a cost of $20,000 but we prefer a BMW worth $100,000, then the car cost us $20,000 and the demonstration of our social position cost us an extra $80,000.

One of the weaknesses in this sort of signalling, of course, is that it's always possible to cheat. People can buy houses, cars and access to private schools by borrowing more than they can afford. When you look down a street at the houses and the cars parked in their drives, what you don't see is the size of the owners' debts—nor the impoverished family life caused by the stress and absences of parents who work too hard. Just one of the consequences of recessions is that they sometimes bring out into the open financial overcommitments.

What could relieve the position? What could allow me to catch up with my commitments or, if I've been more disciplined, allow me to move to a higher level of positional display? I know, how about giving me a pay rise that's a lot higher than what everyone else is getting? Many of us are attracted to the idea of increases in our relative income—pay rises that, because they go to us and not to others, help us get ahead of the pack.

It suits economists to see the greater reported happiness of higher income-earners as evidence that money buys happiness. And there's no doubt that to some extent it does. It remains highly likely, however, that the other reason people with higher incomes tend to be happier—a little happier, that is—is because both they and others regard them as of higher status and treat them accordingly.

A study by Rafael Di Tella, an economist at Harvard Business School, and two other economists examined individual panel data on the happiness of 7800 people living in Germany from 1984 to 2000. They found that, over the longer term, increases in status are more powerful (by a factor of almost three) than increases in income in raising happiness. This was because increases in income were more affected by adaptation than increases in status were.

When some economists seek to explain America's lack of increase in happiness over the past 35 years in terms of the widening in income inequality—that is, the lion's share of the increase in national income over that period has gone to very high income-earners—they're tacitly admitting that rises in relative incomes diminish as much wellbeing as they increase. Happiness research suggests that happiness is higher in countries with less unequal distributions of income.

But why do we never learn?

All this raises an obvious question: if income (and the stuff we use it to buy) is subject to such rapidly diminishing marginal utility—if its addition to our happiness is so quickly reduced by adaptation and rising aspirations—why do so many of us persist in pursuing it with such single-mindedness?

Daniel Gilbert, psychologist at Harvard and author of *Stumbling on Happiness*, puts it like this: 'Social relationships are a powerful predictor of happiness—much more so than money is. Happy people have extensive social networks and good relationships with the people in those networks. What's interesting to me is that while money is weakly and complexly correlated with happiness, and social relationships are strongly and simply correlated with happiness, most of us spend most of our time trying to be happy by pursuing wealth. Why?'

It's a good question. Let me offer a range of answers from different psychologists, which don't so much conflict as answer the question at different levels.

Two professors from the University of Exeter, Stephen Lea and Paul Webley, argue that human behaviour towards money can't solely be explained by its usefulness—its ability to buy the things we want—because it also has a more addictive quality. It's like a drug. They offer five examples of money's extra-monetary qualities. First, money looms large in our minds—literally. Separate studies have shown that children perceive money to be physically larger than it actually is, and that at one time of high inflation people thought that old pound notes were physically bigger than the new ones when, in reality, they were the same size.

Second, the real value of money diminishes continuously because of continuing inflation. But people perpetually fail to take this into account, suffering from what economists call 'money illusion'. Many Europeans were flummoxed by the introduction of the euro. Studies have shown that people tend to overestimate the true value of money that has a higher face value and underestimate the real value of money that has a lower face value.

Third, people are attached to the form that money takes and will often resist changes. The Brits have resisted the introduction of the euro, and Americans continue to reject the replacement of dollar bills with dollar coins. Fourth, people have an emotional relationship with money, either loving or hating it. Fifth, as part of our emotional attitude there are times when it can't be used—money often isn't acceptable as a gift and almost never in sexual relationships. Talk of money is frowned on in connection with high art, religion and education.

The authors argue that money isn't just a tool but also acts as a drug on the mind, changing how we feel. Part of the benefit people derive from acquiring money—feeling good—doesn't lead to any actual benefit in the world. So we chase money partly just for the sake of having it.

Richard Easterlin, the economic historian, says time spent in the pursuit of income takes away from the time available for family, exercise and recreation. The net balance—more time pursuing income, less time for family and recreation—tends to reduce our happiness. So why do we do it? Because of our inability to foresee the way the change in our aspirations arising from the time we devote to money matters will lead us to spend too little time on family and health. The result is a substitution of goods (stuff) for time spent with spouse and family.

The Dieners remind us that there's a difference between wanting something, even wanting it very much, and liking it once you have it. We've all seen that when children beg their parents for a pet or a guitar, but quickly lose interest once it's been acquired. Adults are subject to the same failing. Drugs such as nicotine can produce the same effect—we crave another cigarette even though we don't much enjoy smoking. And sometimes it works the other way: we studiously avoid something only to find that, when eventually we try it, we enjoy it.

How do these mismatches occur? As we saw in Chapter 2, neuroscientists say the brain has separate systems for wanting and liking. If so, it's not surprising they can get out of synch. The Dieners observe that the discrepancy between wanting and liking is a reason the economists' model of wellbeing based on people's market choices is not a perfect guide to happiness.

Daniel Kahneman, the Nobel laureate, Alan Krueger, an economist also from Princeton, and three psychologists investigated why so many people have an exaggerated belief in the ability of more income to increase their happiness. They attribute it largely to 'focusing illusion'—our tendency to attribute greater importance to factors that just happen to be in our minds when we're asked vague questions such as how satisfied we are with our lives.

The researchers' own explanation of why income has a weak effect on happiness is that, as income rises, the way people use their time doesn't shift towards those activities associated with better feelings. People with greater income tend to devote relatively more time to work, compulsory non-work activities (such as shopping and childcare) and active leisure (such as exercise) and less time to passive leisure (such as watching television or just relaxing).

In contrast, when people think about how more income would affect their happiness, they probably see themselves devoting more time to leisure pursuits such as watching a big-screen plasma television or playing golf.

So far we've had psychological explanations of why our attitudes to money are off-beam. Now Jonah Lehrer, an American neuroscience journalist and blogger, suggests what may be happening inside our brains when we experience adaptation and aspiration. Once we purchase something, we automatically start taking it for granted and begin yearning for something new.

This phenomenon is built into the brain at a most basic level. Wolfram Schultz, a neuroscientist at Cambridge University, has spent the last few decades measuring the firing rates of dopamine neurons in the brains of monkeys. He sounds a loud tone, waits for a few seconds, and then squirts a few ounces of fruit juice into the monkey's mouth. At first, the dopamine neurons don't fire until the juice is delivered and the monkey doesn't feel happy until he gets the reward.

However, once the animal learns that the tone usually predicts the imminent arrival of juice, the same neurons begin firing at the sound of the tone instead of waiting for the sweet reward. The noise now triggers the same burst of pleasure that was once reserved for the juice; it's become a 'neural proxy' for the expected reward. When monkeys hear the tone and expect juice but none arrives, their dopamine neurons fire at a very low, disappointed rate.

So this neural system is about *anticipation*. Our cells are constantly adapting to happiness, lavishing their bursts of chemical pleasure instead onto our *expectations* of pleasure. As soon as we enjoy the juice we begin to ignore it and start looking for the next pleasurable thing.

But, Jonah argues, dopaminergic adaptation explains why it's so hard to buy happiness. We also need to explain why all our wealth can also make us sad. A big part of the problem is conspicuous consumption, he says. When someone wears a Rolex watch they don't make themselves happier—their dopamine neurons have already adapted to the luxury good— but they do manage to raise the expectations of everybody wearing less expensive watches. These people now feel inferior because their Timex or Casio has been devalued by the costlier item.

Multiply this phenomenon across a full range of consumer products—from clothes to cars, stereos to shoes—and you begin to see why there's so much depression in developed countries. Not only do people's dopamine neurons automatically adapt to their level of income, but those same neurons are constantly being bombarded with a new set of expectations. Many of these expectations are bound to be unfulfilled—we can't all wear Rolexes—and so we end up feeling like a monkey that's heard the tone but not got any juice.

So far in our attempt to explain why we keep getting it wrong—repeating behaviour we ought to have learnt doesn't work—we've really only got to explanations of *how* we get it wrong; how the mechanism works, even to the point of explaining how it happens at the level of the chemicals being released in our brains. We haven't yet reached the point of explaining *why* we have such a mechanism when it leads us to go on behaving in unsatisfying ways. For that deeper level we need to go back to Dan Gilbert.

Individuals and societies don't have the same fundamental need, he says. Individuals want to be happy, and societies want individuals to consume. Most of us don't feel personally responsible for stoking our country's economic engine; we feel personally responsible for increasing our own wellbeing. These different goals present a dilemma, and society cunningly solves it by teaching us that consumption will bring us happiness.

Society convinces us that what's good for the economy is good for us, too. It does so mainly through advertising. We live in the shadow of a great lie, and by the time we figure out that it *is* a lie we are closing in on death and have become irrelevant consumers, a new generation of young and relevant consumers takes our place in the great chain of shopping.

Wow. Interesting thought. It's saying that, at base, it's marketing and advertising that keeps us pounding away on the hedonic treadmill when there are more satisfying things we could be doing. Well, maybe. But, as I'll discuss in Chapter 9, I don't accept that using advertising to con us into consuming more than we need to make us happy is the only way society could organise its economy and find employment for all those who want to work.

Materialism

As physical beings we are part of the material world and need to build our tangible resources to experience security and comfort, the Dieners remind us. But we're also spiritual beings, needing a sense of meaning and purpose that's larger than ourselves and that connects us to humanity and nature. And we're also psychological beings who interpret the world around us, and this means our happiness depends partly on the mental habits we develop.

So the material is inescapable. Even were we to take vows of poverty, chastity and silence, we'd still need food to eat, clothes to wear, somewhere to shelter from the weather, and much else. We have to come to terms with the material, and most of us reach a deal that's more comfortable than a monk's. We're all materialists to a greater or lesser extent, but the extent matters.

The Dieners define materialism as 'wanting money and material goods more than you want other things, such as love or leisure time'. If that's you, the psychologists have bad news. The point is that, as with so many things in life, it's a matter of getting the balance right. And I suspect a lot of us haven't.

I've long believed we're living in an era of heightened materialism. David Myers, the leading psychology textbook author, says the American Dream has become life, liberty and the purchase of happiness.

The American Freshman Survey has polled the attitudes of students entering tertiary education throughout the United States since 1967. In that year, 42 per cent of freshers said it was very important to be 'very well off financially'. By 2005, the proportion believing this reached a record high of 71 per cent. Over the same period, the proportion saying it was very important or essential for them to 'develop a meaningful philosophy of life' fell from 86 per cent to 52 per cent.

I doubt if the Australian Dream is much different. It's possible the global financial crisis and the consequent Great Recession will bring the era of heightened materialism to an end, but if so I'll be pleasantly surprised.

The dominant ideology of economic rationalism is both an effect and a cause of our greater materialism. The politicians started listening to the advice of economists because they believed (correctly) it would yield the higher material standards of living they believed (possibly incorrectly) the electorate was demanding. But once we moved to that more economically 'rational' world, monetary incentives and material objectives became more prominent in our thinking.

A study by Kathleen Vohs, of the University of Minnesota, and colleagues looked at how money, and even reminders of money, affected people. They 'primed' the concept of money by leaving subtle reminders around the laboratory, such as a flying dollar screen saver and a framed dollar bill on the wall. Remarkably, these small cues led subjects to feel more self-confident. They also were able to persevere with difficult tasks longer than the control group.

Fine. But they were less likely to be sociable later on, preferring to wait for the experimenters alone rather than with others, sitting further away from others in the waiting room and opting for solitary rather than group activities when offered the choice. They were also less helpful to a confederate who appeared to have dropped his belongings, and they donated less of their earnings from the experiment to charity when given the opportunity to do so.

After that it shouldn't come as a surprise that possessing materialist values has been shown to be a strong predictor of unhappiness. People who agree with statements such as 'you will buy things just because you want them' tend to be less satisfied with life, more likely to be depressed, more likely to be paranoid and more likely to be narcissistic.

A study by some of the biggest names in the psychology of happiness, Carol Nickerson, Norbert Schwarz, Ed Diener and Daniel Kahneman, took more than 12,000 students who entered various big-name, academically selective American universities in 1976 and asked them to rate 'the importance to you personally of being very well off financially'. In 1997 the same people—by then in their late thirties—were asked the amount of their household income and how they rated their satisfaction with various aspects of their lives.

The study found that, almost invariably, the stronger a person's desire for financial success, the less satisfied they were with their lives overall. Taking the case of people on US$25,000 a year, those who regarded financial success as not important tended to be 6 percentage points happier than those regarding it as essential. Those with strong material aspirations were least satisfied with their family life and friendships, as well as having lower job satisfaction. But it turns out that satisfaction with family life and with your job are the strongest predictors of overall satisfaction with life.

Perhaps the greatest specialist in the study of materialism is Tim Kasser, a psychologist at Knox College, Illinois and author of *The High Price of Materialism*. Tim defines materialist values as giving highest emphasis to the pursuit of money, possessions, personal appearance or fame and popularity. People with less materialistic values give highest emphasis to self-acceptance and personal growth, intimacy and friendship, or contribution to society.

Tim refers to materialistic values as 'extrinsic'—they involve seeking satisfaction outside yourself. Such people tend to be possessive (they prefer to own rather than rent and don't like throwing stuff away), 'non-generous' and envious. They also watch a lot of television—which makes them worse. They report more symptoms of anxiety, are at greater risk of depression and experience more frequent physical irritations. They use more alcohol and drugs and have more impoverished personal relationships. Even their dreams seem infected with anxiety and distress.

Sonja Lyubomirsky offers several reasons why materialism doesn't make us happy. Even when people finally attain their materialistic goals the achievement doesn't translate into an increase in happiness. Materialistic people have been found to hold unrealistically high expectations of what material things can do for them. Materialism may distract people from the relatively more meaningful and joyful aspects of life, such as nurturing their relationships, enjoying the present and contributing to their community.

The rich are different

F. Scott Fitzgerald is said to have remarked to Ernest Hemingway that 'the very rich are different from you and me'. 'Yes,' Hemingway replied, 'they have more money.' But research comes down more on Fitzgerald's side. According to the Dieners, America has about 8 million millionaires—though I guess the global financial crisis may have cut that number by now. Of course, in Australia it doesn't take a lot to scrape in as a multi-millionaire. Anyone with a home in Sydney or Perth they own outright, plus reasonable superannuation savings, can muster $2 million.

But when, in the mid-1980s, Ed Diener and colleagues sent questionnaires to 100 of those named in the Forbes list of the richest Americans—and got replies from almost half of them—they found they were just a bit more satisfied than ordinary souls. These were people with a net worth of at least US$125 million—the owners of jets, private islands, and so forth. But they explained their happiness very much in terms of pleasing family relationships, helping the world, and pride and fulfilment from their work.

One respect in which the rich are different is that they save a much higher proportion of their income than you and I do. Why—because they have so much money? It's not that simple, as Christopher Carroll, an economics professor at Johns Hopkins University in Baltimore, makes clear in a paper. Economists measure saving as the part of your income that you don't spend on consumption, and they define saving as 'deferred consumption'.

The thing is that, in conventional economics, the only rational reason for going to the hassle (the 'dis-utility') of earning an income is so you can enjoy the utility that comes from consuming the proceeds. Consumption is the aim of the game. So, though you may not wish to consume all your income now, you're just saving some to spend later. Why else would you bother?

Actually, the theory does get a little more sophisticated. The 'permanent income hypothesis' says that people will gear their consumption not just to their current income, but also to the income level they expect to enjoy in the future. So a young doctor may consume more than a young boilermaker, even though their current incomes are similar. There'll be times when a person's consumption will exceed their current income, and others when they consume less than their current income (and so save) because their income is temporarily high.

Another theory that can be combined with this is the idea of 'life-cycle saving'. People try to keep their consumption reasonably smooth over the course of their lives, so they'll save up part of their income during their working life so they've got something to live on when they're too old to work. And, of course, there's the 'precautionary motive' for saving. People put something away because they never know when they might lose their job or have a lot of medical expenses.

Now, here's Christopher's point—his first one, anyway. When you construct a mathematical model using these various theories and compare its results with the actual figures for people's saving in the United States, you find the model greatly under-predicts the amount of wealth held by the very wealthiest households.

Remember that wealth is just accumulated saving, even if some of it has come from capital gains (because these are a form of income)—though, of course, wealth may include money saved by others and acquired through inheritance. Remember, too, that we're talking the wealthiest 1 per cent of households. So it's the filthy rich—strictly public company chief executives and above.

So the conventional theory is quite inadequate to explain the very high rate of saving by the rich. The life-cycle theory predicts that people will aim to have consumed all their savings by the time they cark it. But, though it's hard to know when you'll go—and so how much you'll be needing—the very rich die with infinitely more than can be explained by a bit of precautionary overshooting.

OK, so maybe we need to allow for the pleasure ('utility') the rich derive from leaving as much wealth as possible to their kids. Sorry. Attempts to take account of this 'bequest motive'—the 'dynastic' model and the 'joy of giving' model—don't cut it either. In various surveys of the elderly and even the elderly rich, surprisingly few list inheritance among their 'five top reasons for saving'. What's more, the *childless* elderly rich show little sign of running down their savings either.

Obviously, it's time for Chris to wheel out his own theory. Max Weber, the guy who dreamt up the Protestant Work Ethic, argued a long time ago that the pursuit of wealth for its own sake was the 'spirit of capitalism'. So Carroll calls it his Capitalist Spirit model: the reason the very rich save so much is that they, unlike the rest of us, derive utility *directly* from the ownership of wealth.

Now, this makes them sound like misers who enjoy sitting up at night counting their money—or diving into swimming pools of the stuff like Scrooge McDuck. But Chris has a much better way of explaining it. He contends that the marginal utility of consumption decreases sharply with the level of consumption. Particularly if you define consumption strictly as the consumption of *non-durable* goods and services, it's easy to see how someone with a huge income would have neither the inclination nor the time to consume more than a fraction of it. Take Bill Gates, for instance. At one stage his net worth was said to be US$40 billion. Assuming he earns a 10 per cent annual rate of return on his wealth, he'd have to spend US$4 billion a year—or more than US$10 million a day—on non-durable goods and services simply to avoid accumulating any further wealth.

If the seriously rich derive so little marginal utility from plebeian consumption, they have to find some alternative way to employ their wealth, the marginal utility from which decreases more slowly—thus making the alternative a kind of 'luxury good'. Now, the luxury goods generally associated with the wealthy are such things as art, jewellery, flash estates and even sports teams.

See the point? All those things are *assets*—they don't count as consumption, they count as wealth. When you're filthy rich, even your luxury indulgences don't reduce your wealth.

But if you still don't like the notion of the rich deriving utility directly from the ownership of wealth, Chris thinks it's pretty much the same thing to say the utility comes *indirectly*, either from the activities that lead to wealth accumulation or from a flow of services that's closely tied to the ownership of that wealth.

Starting with the latter, what services could flow from the ownership of wealth? Well, the obvious one is power. Howard Hughes said, 'Money is the measuring rod of power', and there's any number of quotes to the same effect. But I prefer the idea that the rich derive utility from the activities that lead to greater wealth. This says the rich enjoy doing their jobs well and they view the accumulation of wealth as the principal measure of job performance. According to the US businessman H.L. Hunt, at one time the world's richest man, 'Money's just a way of keeping score—it's the game that matters.' Just so. I reckon, to these guys, it's just a big, competitive, exciting game in which one dollar counts as one point.

And we should add a refinement suggested by Robert Frank, an economics professor at Cornell University and author of *Luxury Fever*. Bob argues that an intrinsic component of human nature is a tendency to judge yourself by comparison with others (whereas conventional economics assumes we never do that, but focus solely on personal bests). So having lots of wealth matters because it's an index of social status. If you wonder what it is that drives men such as Frank Lowy and Rupert Murdoch, I think we've put our finger on it.

Where to shop

A bumper sticker says, People who think money doesn't buy happiness just don't know the right shops. There's more truth to that quip than you might think. Growing research evidence suggests that one of the reasons our ever-rising income doesn't make us any happier is because we're spending it on the wrong things.

As long ago as 1976, the economist Tibor Scitovsky of Stanford wrote in his classic *The Joyless Economy* that there was an important distinction between consumer spending aimed at comfort and that aimed at stimulation. Spending on comfort goods—such as homes and cars—is soon subject to hedonic adaptation, eventually creating dependence and addiction. But spending on creativity and novelty—such as music, literature and the arts—yields more pleasurable arousal because it is less subject to adaptation.

Research suggests we're more likely to overestimate the utility we'll derive from physical goods and purchases serving our extrinsic material desires—that is, purchases intended to impress other people—and underestimate the utility from those satisfying intrinsic needs—stuff we want for its own sake—and our social needs. We tend to spend more than we should on goods and activities that give us a quick thrill and less than we should on stuff where the thrill is more moderate but longer lasting.

Thomas Gilovich and Leaf Van Boven, both psychologists at Cornell University, have found that 'experiential purchases'—those made with the intention of acquiring a life experience—make people happier than ordinary material purchases. The good life is more about doing things than having things, they say. This is because experiences improve with time; we tend to remember the good bits and forget the bad bits, and can even laugh about things we found frightening or shocking at the time. Experiences are less susceptible than goods are to unfavourable social comparisons. And experiences have more social value; they bring us into more contact with people than the goods we buy, and it's more socially acceptable for us to talk about our experiences than about our possessions.

In his book *Authentic Happiness* Martin Seligman, a psychologist at the University of Pennsylvania, warns against pursuing 'shortcuts to pleasure' such as drugs, chocolate, loveless sex, shopping, masturbation, television and spectator sport. There's nothing wrong with most of these things, it's just that the pleasure they give is terribly brief. The trouble with them is that they're too easy. They require little effort on our part, and it's the things that do require some effort that we find more satisfying.

Then there's the question of our attitude towards the shopping we do. In *The Paradox of Choice* Barry Schwartz, a psychologist from Swarthmore College, Philadelphia, advises us to be 'satisficers', not maximisers. A maximiser seeks and accepts only the best. You seek to assure that every decision or purchase is the best that could be made. A satisficer, by contrast, is a person who settles for something that's good enough and doesn't worry about the possibility that there may be something better.

This doesn't mean you accept the first thing you see—you do have standards—but it does mean you don't devote hours and days to the search for perfection. Why accept less than the best? Because it's impossible to know when you've found the best. Maximisers are often haunted by the fear that somewhere out there is something better than the best they've found so far.

Maximisers are always comparing what they bought with what others bought. They tend to get less satisfaction from what they buy and suffer more regret about what they bought. People with high maximisation scores on a test Barry developed experience less satisfaction with life, are less optimistic and more depressed than people with low maximisation scores. Of course, this is only a correlation, but Barry believes being a maximiser does play a causal role in people's unhappiness.

Someone who's convinced that how people spend their money is important to their happiness is Elizabeth Dunn, a social psychologist at the University of British Columbia. With some colleagues, she demonstrated that spending money on other people makes you happier than spending money on yourself. In one study she found that employees who devoted more of their bonus payments to 'pro-social spending' (buying something for someone else or making a donation to charity) experienced greater happiness after receiving the bonus. The manner in which they spent the bonus was a stronger predictor of their happiness than the actual size of bonus.

What to take away

Money is important. We couldn't survive without it and it *is* better to be rich than to be poor. But after we've satisfied our basic needs, money's ability to make us happier diminishes rapidly. Other factors—particularly our relationships—have a much bigger effect on our wellbeing, and if we allow a preoccupation with money to crowd out our relationships we lose on the deal. So it's a question of balance and priorities, not taking a vow of poverty.

Acquiring more money does less to increase our happiness than we expect it to because we so quickly adapt to it and the things it will buy, because our aspirations keep running ahead of our incomes and because social comparison—keeping up with the Joneses—is like an arms race. Other aspects of our lives have a stronger and more lasting effect on our happiness because they're less susceptible to adaptation, aspiration and social comparison.

Adaptation is less complete in the cases of family circumstances and health than it is in the case of material goods. Social comparison is less powerful in family life and health than in the purchase of material goods because family and health are less accessible to public scrutiny. Aristotle said wealth is a means to an end, whereas friendship is an end in itself. Someone else said that the things we really want can't be purchased in the market.

The Dieners say each of us must ask ourselves whether we have become a victim of our rising material desires. More important than the size of your pay cheque or your net worth is your attitude towards your money and the ways in which you spend it. Rich people who spend beyond their means feel poor, whereas people who live within a careful budget feel secure. Regardless of your actual income, it is your material aspirations that colour your mood.

The research about the effect of money says that it's generally good for your happiness to *have* money, but toxic to your happiness to *want* money too much. The Dieners' antidote to excessive emphasis on money is to introduce the notion of 'psychological wealth'—which includes all the resources a person needs to live a good life. It's 'your true total net worth'.

Besides money—'material sufficiency to meet our needs'—a number of other resources are essential to our happiness: loving and supportive relationships, engaging activities and work, positive attitudes and emotions, physical and mental health, values and life goals to achieve them, and spirituality and meaning in life.

Money can be a help in attaining psychological wealth, but it must be considered in the bigger picture of what makes people genuinely rich.

5

WORK AND HAPPINESS

I love humanity; it's people I can't stand.
— An economist's lament

I love my job. I find it utterly absorbing and satisfying. Of course, that's easy for me to say—I have the best job in the world, being paid a fortune to sit in an armchair and pass judgement on how other people are doing their jobs, starting with the prime minister. But I'd like to think that's not the only reason I'm convinced there are few aspects of our lives more important than the work we do.

Between them, the economists and the business people have got work wrong, though they make opposite mistakes. The economists consider leisure to be good (because it yields 'utility' or satisfaction) and work to be bad (because it yields 'dis-utility'). Their model assumes people work purely for the money (because it can be used to buy the goods and services that do yield utility). Wrong.

On the other hand, business people—or those who do the talking for them—consider work to be good and leisure bad.

They're always trying to make us feel guilty about four weeks'
annual leave—four weeks!—and are always trying to persuade
the politicians to cut away at public holidays. Wrong. Neither the
annual leave we take nor the public holidays we get are excessive
by the standards of other developed countries. If we work as
hard as we do, surely we're entitled to a few recreational breaks.
The simple truth is that *both* work and leisure are good. The trick
is to get the right balance between them, and do a far bit of both.

Why? Because both should add to our satisfaction. But let's
focus on work. It seems clear that humans are a working animal.
We've been designed to work and—assuming we're of working
age—if we don't work we're unlikely to be very happy. In any
case, since most of us have to work—including, of course, stay-
at-home mums, who do plenty of work, they just don't get paid
cash for it—it's worth doing all we can to ensure we enjoy it.

In his latest book *The Pleasures and Sorrows of Work*, Alain de
Botton argues that though 'all societies have had work at their
centre, ours is the first to suggest that it could be something
much more than a punishment or a penance'. This is a relatively
new idea, he says, that can be traced back to the European bour-
geois thinkers of the 18th century, who turned the old idea that
work was toil into the modern concept that paid work is the
realm of significance and meaning.

Really? I find that very hard to believe. We've had to work for
our living since before we descended from the trees, but the idea
of taking pride in your work and deriving satisfaction from it is
a notion invented in the 18th century? Evolutionary psychologists tell us we've evolved in such a way that our desire for
happiness serves to motivate us to do those things that help us
to survive and reproduce. Since work is essential to our survival,
it makes evolutionary sense for work to make us feel good.

And even if Alain was right and the notion of job satisfaction is a relatively recent affectation, I'd be unrepentant: if the purpose of human civilisation is to improve the human lot, why stop at en suite bathrooms and high-definition television? Why not add to the list the wish that we might enjoy our jobs?

Jobs are satisfying

The simple truth is that most of us do enjoy our jobs. According to a survey conducted by Sydney University's Workplace Research Centre in the early 2000s, more than 70 per cent of Australian workers are very satisfied with the quality of their working lives. This is pretty much in line with survey results in other developed countries. This survey found that satisfaction was highest among younger workers, but declined somewhat as workers got older. (The pattern in other rich countries is for job satisfaction to be U-shaped, with younger and older workers more satisfied than those in their mid-thirties.)

A survey conducted in Britain by Andrew Oswald, professor of economics at Warwick University, found that those who work for non-profit organisations were the most satisfied workers, with the self-employed enjoying their jobs more than the employed. Andrew also found that pay has an effect on job satisfaction—not its absolute amount, however, but relative pay: how what I get compares with what others are getting. And having qualifications greater than needed for a job is associated with discontent.

For reasons psychologists don't understand, the British survey found that women tend to be more satisfied with their jobs than men. When you consider that men tend to have better jobs than women, with more pay and higher occupational status, this is surprising. One possibility is that women have lower expectations, but my suspicion is that they see themselves as volunteers more than men do.

According to Tom Smith, director of America's regular General Social Survey, conducted by the National Opinion Research Centre at the University of Chicago, the top dozen occupations yielding the most job satisfaction include clergy, on a score of 87 per cent, firefighters on 80, physical therapists 78, special education teachers 70, other teachers 69, and painters and sculptors on 67. The dozen occupations yielding the least job satisfaction include bartenders on 26 per cent, cashiers on 25, clothing salespeople, hand-packers and food preparers, all on 24, and labourers on 21.

Tom says the most satisfying jobs are mostly professional, especially those involving caring for, teaching or protecting others, and creative pursuits. The least satisfying occupations are mostly low-skill, manual and service jobs, especially customer service and food and beverage preparation and serving.

Another way of getting at the extent of job satisfaction is to ask people if they would still work if it became financially unnecessary. Michael Argyle, psychology professor at Oxford, interpreted a British survey along these lines as showing that 30 to 40 per cent of workers really like their jobs, a similar group would keep working but would try to change their jobs, and 25 to 30 per cent don't really enjoy their work.

Looking at job satisfaction from yet another perspective, Michael notes the results of an old and possibly outdated study asking people in different occupations whether they'd choose the work again. Mathematicians came top with 91 per cent of them saying yes. Then it was lawyers with 83 per cent, journalists 82, skilled printers 52, and skilled car and steel workers 41. Last were unskilled steel workers, with only 16 per cent of them saying they'd do it all again.

This suggests that job satisfaction tends to be higher the more highly skilled the job is. Job *status* is determined by a combination of factors: pay, conditions of work and skills required. But the correlation between job status and job satisfaction is surprisingly low.

Of course, some part of the variation in people's job satisfaction is attributable to genetic factors. Some research suggests inherited personality differences account for about 30 per cent of the variation.

Job satisfaction and overall happiness

It's obvious that people who enjoy their jobs will be enjoying a big chunk of their lives—for a full-timer, work accounts for about a third of our waking hours—so it's no surprise that those who enjoy their work tend to be happier. Sonja Lyubomirsky, author of *The How of Happiness*, was surprised to find, in a study she did with Ed Diener and another colleague, that one factor towered over relationships in its connection with happiness: work.

Tom Smith of America's General Social Survey confirms that job satisfaction and general happiness are positively related, with those saying they are very happy in general rising from less than 16 per cent among those very dissatisfied with their job to more than 45 per cent among those very satisfied with their job.

So while most of the occupations whose practitioners rank high in general happiness are professions involving help to others, technical and scientific expertise or creativity, and the occupations with the least happy people are mostly unskilled manual and service positions, there are some notable exceptions.

Physicians are first in occupational *prestige*, but don't make the top 12 in general happiness. Lawyers rank second in occupational prestige, but don't make the happiness top 12 either.

In a survey he conducted in 2003 in conjunction with the Australian Unity Wellbeing Index, Bob Cummins, of Deakin University, found that non-earning men aged 26 to 55 showed significantly lower wellbeing than earning men, suggesting the importance of work to men of this age range. More generally, we know how important work is to happiness from the very low wellbeing scores of people who are unemployed, with their lowness greater than can be explained simply by their loss of income.

Research by the Australian Council for Educational Research showed that full-time workers are notably happier with their lives than those who are part time. This may be simply because they'd like to be earning more, but it's at least as likely that more work would itself make them happier.

Too much of a good thing

I'm a believer in hard work, mainly because I believe it's a source of so much satisfaction. I work a lot longer than 40 hours a week, and am happy to pile the work on the young journalists who work with me up until the point where they become parents. In their book *Happiness*, Ed Diener and his son Robert Biswas-Diener say it's true that successful people in general, and calling-oriented workers in particular (that's me), often work hard and spend long hours on the job.

However, it *is* possible to work too hard. And although the notion that we're *all* working much longer hours than we used to is mistaken, it's true that more people are working very long hours.

It's possible some people work exceptional hours because they gain so much intrinsic satisfaction from the work they do, but my impression is that workaholism is motivated mainly by a desire for pay rises and promotions. I also suspect that sometimes long hours represent a preference for the office over a home where relations aren't as warm as they ought to be. There are probably some men—and maybe some women—who believe their family's financial commitments leave them with little choice but to work long hours.

One reason for suspecting the motives of workaholics is the obvious but oft-neglected truth that our personal efficiency reduces significantly once we work too many hours and aren't getting enough mental and physical rest and recreation. These days most jobs have an important quality component. Working excessive hours is unlikely to impress bosses if it doesn't lead to a superior performance.

People sometimes inquire sardonically, whatever happened to all the extra leisure time the futurologists promised us back in the 1970s? The implication is either that the seers got it terribly wrong or some dastardly powers-that-be have cheated us out of it. Actually, it's not that simple.

For a start, the futurologists were right in predicting that the spread of computerisation and other labour-saving technology would make it possible for goods and services to be produced using less labour time. In other words, the productivity of labour—output per hour of labour input—has grown strongly over the past 40 years. As a nation, we—along with all the developed nations—had a choice of whether to take that increased productiveness in the form of fewer working hours or higher real wages.

As a nation—like most other nations—we opted for the

higher incomes rather than the shorter hours. Rather than choosing more time for leisure we preferred more money to buy stuff. Why? Partly, I suspect, because most of us quite enjoy work. Also, perhaps, because we weren't sure what we'd do with any extra leisure time. Mihaly Csikszentmihalyi, the psychologist whose discovery of 'flow' we'll get to in a minute, has concluded from his research that 'we all want to have more free time, but when we get it we don't know what to do with it'.

(Answer: stay active. Our need to work probably explains why we find active leisure more satisfying than passive leisure. It would certainly explain why volunteering is so popular—particularly among the retired—and so rewarding. Most people are happier gardening than sitting in a speed boat, or talking to friends than watching television.)

The stronger explanation, however, is that we opted for more money rather than more leisure because we live in an era of heightened materialism. The illusion that acquiring more and more stuff will make us happy is particularly strong. You may argue that this was a choice foisted on us by business, economists and politicians. There is logic to this: the longer we work the more goods and services we produce, thus making the economy grow faster—something each of those groups is convinced is a good thing.

But I'm never willing to accept the argument that you and I are powerless cogs in the capitalist machine, at the mercy of the nefarious wishes of the powers-that-be. Sorry, that's a cop out. For social trends to emerge in a market economy, conditions have to be right on both the supply side and the demand side. Greedy bosses and deluded economists wanted us to produce and consume more, but we took little persuading. Had we put up much resistance, popularly elected governments would have wanted to protect us by legislating for a shorter working week. The union movement's silence on the issue suggests it was in no doubt about its members' preference for the money rather than the beach box.

Work–life balance

One respect in which we undoubtedly have been working longer hours is that the amount of paid work per household has increased as women have greatly increased their involvement in the paid labour force. I've never accepted that this remarkable social trend is driven primarily by the difficulty families have had coping with the rising cost of living.

I think the most fundamental cause of women's increased participation in the paid workforce is a change in the attitudes of parents, sometime in the 1960s, that girls were as much entitled to an education as their brothers. Girls have taken to education so well in the subsequent decades that they now slightly outnumber (and outperform) boys in Year 12 and at university.

With young women as a class now being highly educated—at no little cost to their parents, the government and themselves—it's not in the least surprising that they should want the intellectual gratification, social standing and income that come from putting their qualifications to work in the paid labour force.

This, perhaps the most significant social change of our era, requires major change to arrangements and attitudes in the labour market that business and governments are yet to fully come to terms with. I'll have more to say about that when we get to the discussion of government policy in Chapter 9.

But it shouldn't surprise you to know that I'm not willing to simply categorise the issue of work–life balance as a problem 'they'—politicians and business people—should do something to fix. To *some* extent it's a problem of our own making and our own choosing.

At the family level the problem is not one of the high *cost* of living but of the high cost of maintaining a high *standard* of living. When the very first wives decided to take paid employment—or to return to paid employment earlier following childbirth—it must have occurred to those couples that this would give them an advantage over their peers in terms of the size of the mortgage repayments and other spending they now could afford.

As other couples joined them in becoming two-income families, however, their advantage would have been lost in the general increase in what younger married couples could afford. A fair bit of the couples' increased purchasing power would have translated into higher prices for the sorts of homes young families typically live in. So what began as a material advantage to those couples where the wife was willing to go out to work eventually became a constraint on the freedom of couples where the wife preferred to stay at home with the kids. This option now comes at the price of being willing to accept a standard of living a little lower than their peers.

(I say a little lower because, for many women earning hourly wage rates that are less than stellar, the *net* monetary gain from paid work is less than you might expect, after taking account of childcare costs, travel and business clothing costs, and all the costs of paying others to help with the housework, including the cost of pre-prepared and take-away meals. Then there are the non-monetary costs of reduced free leisure time for wives and husbands doing housework after work, or the cost of living with it not done. All this is the obverse of the great but invisible advantage enjoyed by single-income couples: governments have yet to find a way of taxing work performed without money changing hands. In this case the limited net gain to many second-earners supports my earlier argument that they generally don't do paid work just for the money.)

This explains why I'm less than fully convinced by some of the complaints we hear about the difficulty of balancing work and family commitments. It's here we come face to face with a tough choice between our material and our relational aspirations. Leaving to one side the responsibility of governments (which, as I say, I'll get to in Chapter 9), the at-least-partial solution at the level of the individual is obvious: if you're finding the juggling act too hard, reduce the number of balls you have in the air by being willing to accept a lower material standard of living.

Needless to say, this solution applies to husbands as much as wives, especially in those cases where the woman is in fact the primary breadwinner. The limited popularity of 50/52 schemes—where the boss agrees to give you an extra two weeks of unpaid leave a year, then divides the remaining 50 weeks by 52 so as to smooth out the loss of income—also makes me suspect that some complaints about overwork aren't fair dinkum.

If your conscience was troubling you over your decision to opt for money over family, how would you rationalise it to yourself? More particularly, how would you explain your choice to a pollster asking you questions about work–life balance? You'd carry on about how bad you felt that external forces were preventing you from seeing more of your family.

Why work makes us happy

Even so, it's clear from all the survey results we've examined so far that they hardly offer support for the assumption implicit in the economists' model that money is the only motivation for paid work. Lesser paid women tend to be more satisfied with their jobs than men are. People working for non-profit organisations are the most satisfied workers, but are hardly well paid.

Clergy, firefighters, teachers, painters and sculptors are the most job-satisfied occupations but, again, hardly the highest paid. Actually, some of the highest paid professions are missing from the top of the job-satisfaction and general-happiness league tables. And then there's the 70 to 75 per cent of workers who say they'd keep working even if they had no financial need to.

So, apart from the money, what are the things about work that give us satisfaction and add to our happiness? In his book *The Pursuit of Happiness*, David Myers nominates four main factors.

First, work gives us personal identity. Our work helps to define us, and most of us are happy to be seen as having the characteristics commonly attributed to our occupation. Journalists are nosy, always asking questions; accountants are careful with money; and economists are cold and rational. Taking our identity from our work is surely nothing new. Consider all those of us whose surname derives of the occupation of an ancestor: Smith, Fletcher, Potter, Miller, Carter, Bishop, Thatcher, Carpenter, Fisher, Archer, Cook, Wright.

Second, work allows us to identify with a community—often, several communities: our workmates, our organisation, our profession. Michael Argyle says social support from co-workers can do a lot to relieve work stress, more even than the support from friends or family outside.

Third, work adds purpose to our lives. It's part of the way we care for those dependent on us and often the main way we seek to make the world a better place. Studs Terkel, the great chronicler of the views of American workers, wrote that work is a search 'for daily meaning as well as daily bread, for recognition as well as cash, for astonishment rather than torpor; in short, for a sort of life rather than a Monday through Friday sort of dying'. Studs describes 'the Chicago piano tuner, who seeks and finds the sound that delights; the bookbinder, who saves a piece of history; the Brooklyn fireman, who saves a piece of life'. One reason I was dissatisfied in my first career as an accountant auditor was I couldn't convince myself that checking people's calculations of the size of their profits was a particularly important thing to do. When I became an economic journalist I had no trouble convincing myself that inflation and unemployment were issues that mattered.

Fourth, work often provides us with a sense of personal control. Indeed, our ability to exercise some control over the way we do our jobs—autonomy, as psychologists call it—has a big effect on how satisfying we find our jobs. Dave Myers says, 'study after study finds that when workers have more control—when they can help define their own goals and hours and when they participate in decision-making—their job satisfaction rises'.

So supervisors are often a source of work discontent. In Andrew Oswald's survey of job satisfaction he found that satisfaction is low in places where the boss controls the pace of work, although it's high in places where customers or colleagues control how fast the work has to be done. This implies that humans don't mind working hard for someone on the same level as themselves, so to speak. It's pressure from above in a hierarchy that upsets them. Michael Argyle says well-being is greater for those who work in teams, especially where levels of co-operation are high, and in autonomous work-groups that can arrange their own work.

On a different tack, the health of those at work is better than for those not at work. In a study that followed 2500 individuals for a year, those in full-time work showed almost no decline in health whereas all the other groups did, including housewives. Work is also good for mental health, which is improved when people start work and gets worse when they stop.

Changing jobs can be a good idea

Although it's no doubt true that, as we saw Sonja Lyubomirsky emphasising in Chapter 3, happiness is best pursued by changing our behaviour rather than our socio-demographic circumstances, I'd make a big exception for changing your job or occupation. When I suffered a midlife crisis at the premature age of 26, and responded by moving from chartered accounting to journalism, I can remember thinking that in journalism I had a greater sense of creativity in a day than I had in a whole year in auditing.

And the experts back up my belief in the importance of finding a job you find truly satisfying. The Dieners list as the first of their factors that produce happiness at work: 'find a job that's the right fit for you'. They quote research conducted by the Swiss psychologist Norbert Semmer on how job dissatisfaction can sometimes be beneficial. Not surprisingly, he found that dissatisfied workers were more likely to quit their jobs and find a new workplace. But he also found that many of the dissatisfied workers were happier in their new workplace, suggesting they weren't simply dyspeptic people who'd be unhappy wherever they worked. So anxiety and frustration in your job can be healthy warning signs to which we should respond.

In your search for a better job, however, take care to avoid what psychologists have dubbed the 'distinction bias'.

Say you're offered two jobs. The first is an interesting job that pays $60,000 a year, while the second is a boring job that pays $70,000 a year. Everything else is equal. The distinction bias predicts that people will consistently overestimate the importance of the $10,000 compared to how interesting the job is and will thus pick the job that will make them miserable.

Why would anyone do something so silly? Materialism? Not in this case. The problem is our limited neural processing power. We have a tendency to focus on the comparisons that are easiest and most obvious—the difference in salaries—rather than on differences that are less tangible and thus less easily measured but which are more important. The antidote is to evaluate the pros and cons of each option separately and only then compare the options with each other. This makes it easier to notice the thing you should most notice: if it's a boring job you're likely to hate it.

How to be happier in your job

But let's say you're not in a position to change your job or occupation, or your degree of dissatisfaction with your present job isn't sufficient to warrant such a major move. There are still plenty of other things you can do to increase your job satisfaction and thus your happiness generally.

A lot of it gets down to attitude—yours. Starting with the obvious, high pay is not the most important cause of job satisfaction. So, if you insist on giving it highest priority, don't be surprised if you don't get much pleasure out of your working life. Sensible choice of occupation puts more emphasis on our abilities, interests and values. Individuals doing voluntary work are often found to be enjoying their work as much or more than paid workers.

The Dieners say happiness at work comes most from two factors: finding a job that's the right fit and working for a company that promotes happiness on the job. That is, one that treats its staff well. That's self-explanatory, so let's look at 'job fit'. Finding a job with the right fit means one involving work that's appropriately challenging, suited to your personality, meaningful and interesting to you.

One of the major themes of the new school of 'positive psychology' is: don't concentrate on correcting your weaknesses, play to your strengths. I guess it's theoretically possible to make ourselves near-perfect by painstakingly eliminating our weak points, but the surest way to happiness and success is just to specialise in the stuff you're good at, the tasks that exploit your 'signature strengths', as the positive psychologists say. How do you discover your greatest strengths? You can do the free test on Professor Martin Seligman's website: www.authentichappiness. sas.upenn.edu.

Suitable jobs should have just the right amount of challenge to fit your abilities. Too much challenge leads to anxiety; too little leads to boredom. In my experience you do need to exercise a bit of courage, however. When my predecessor as economics editor at the *Herald* left, I—being the nearest approximation— was offered the job. I was most uncertain about my ability to fill the big shoes he left. But I remember thinking I'd be a mug not to try my chances. Ever since, I've been more relaxed about putting bright young people into jobs they need to grow into.

Amy Wrzesniewski, professor of organisational behaviour at Yale University, suggests the difference between satisfied and unsatisfied workers turns on how they view their work. People with a 'job orientation' think of their job primarily in terms of its tangible benefits. They're there for the money; they do as they're told but look forward to the end of each shift because they get their kicks from leisure, not work. They'd be prepared to work harder if you offered them a monetary incentive.

By contrast, people with a 'career orientation' enjoy some aspects of their job but not others, and they think a lot about their next holiday. They're motivated by the hope of advancement and status symbols such as bigger offices and better parking spaces. They're prepared to take the initiative in their jobs if they think this will impress their supervisors. They work hard because this will improve their chances of promotion.

But then there are the people with a 'calling orientation'. They love their jobs, feel the work they do is important and believe it makes a contribution to the world. They're motivated by a sense that they're contributing, and think about their work even when they're off the job. They work hard and take the initiative because they find the job intrinsically rewarding.

Obvious question: which type of worker do you think gets most job satisfaction and which type would you prefer to be? According to Amy, about a third of those in any occupation are calling oriented—which means you don't have to be in a fancy 'profession' to have a calling. (When I hire young people to train as economic journalists I say I'm looking for someone 'who's been called by God to be a journalist'—someone with a burning desire to be a reporter, to get her name in the paper, and a willingness to drop whatever salary is necessary to land the job, just as I did years ago.)

In thinking about your own attitude towards your job—whether you have a calling or could possibly acquire one—it's instructive to ponder the distinction between the 'intrinsic' and 'extrinsic' features of jobs. Intrinsic features relate to the nature of the work itself: the possibility to use your skills, the variety of tasks, the opportunity for personal control, whether supervision is supportive or controlling, and the opportunity for contact with other people. By contrast, extrinsic features relate to the background benefits: the pay and fringe benefits, working conditions, job security, physical work security and social status arising from position in the hierarchy or occupational prestige.

You can see that a job orientation focuses solely on the extrinsic factors, whereas the calling orientation focuses on intrinsic factors, with the career orientation being a lot more focused on extrinsic than intrinsic factors.

The moral of the story—one you can find recommended in other aspects of wellbeing—is that if you want to be happy, focus on the intrinsic. Try to get yourself into a job you really enjoy doing for its own sake and do it for your own satisfaction, not because it brings in money, may lead to promotion or just keeps the boss off your back.

Sonja Lyubomirsky says, 'intrinsic goals are those that you pursue because they are inherently satisfying and meaningful to you, which allow you to grow as a person, to develop emotional maturity and to contribute to your community'. She says intrinsic goals add to our happiness because they satisfy our most basic needs for, first, autonomy (feeling we're in control of our behaviour), second, competence (feeling efficacious in dealing with the world around us) and, third, relatedness (feeling satisfied with our interpersonal relationships).

The American social theorist Richard Sennett says we need to reinstate the notion of work as 'craftsmanship', where we can take pleasure in our engagement with the materials and derive satisfaction from experience of a job well done.

People with a calling orientation engage in a practice called 'job crafting'—they take the initiative to change their job in small ways to bring it more into line with their larger vision of what they value in life. This makes their work both more meaningful and more enjoyable. Often they'll be taking it upon themselves to perform tasks no one else is doing, that no one asked them to perform and that they're not paid extra to do. (In a decent workplace, however, when their superiors realise the extra contribution they're making they'll find a way to reward that extra contribution—if not by means of a pay rise then by some informal means, such as giving them greater freedom or taking their advice more seriously.)

Another relevant principle from the general wellbeing literature is that, to wax biblical, you have to lose your life to save it. Robert Frank, an economics professor at Cornell University, wrote in a column for *The New York Times* that those who focus most consciously and intensely on material success tend to experience low levels of measured happiness. 'A far more promising strategy, according to the happiness literature,' he said, 'is to seek work you love. Those who find such a calling typically become deeply engaged in their professional lives. And engagement, in turn, leads to expertise, which in some fields, at least, leads to wealth.

'Finding work that you value for its own sake is thus not only a promising path to happiness, it may also increase your chances of becoming rich. But even if not, it will improve your odds of becoming an interesting person, someone who is attractive to both friends and potential mates alike.'

The unadorned truth is that jobs requiring higher levels of education are likely to be more satisfying (although it remains true that those not intellectually equipped to go far in the education system may well derive more satisfaction from jobs the more highly qualified would find deadly dull). It's true, too, that the 'division of labour'—the division of jobs into ever-more specialised tasks—has made a lot of blue-collar and clerical work more repetitive. The Dieners acknowledge that 'few enjoy work that is always simple or repetitive and has little meaningful purpose'.

Even so, with enough will and imagination it should be possible to craft even jobs such as these to make them more satisfying. One way to do it is to insert more people into them—to become more conscious of the people who are the end-beneficiaries of the work being performed, to have more contact with them or, if nothing else, have more fun with your workmates.

Happiness psychologists like to tell the story of the creative hospital cleaner. In theory, your classic repetitive, unrewarding job. But not in the hands of this lady. She's very aware of the importance of the job she does in helping to combat hospital-borne germs and in keeping the place pleasant for patients, their relatives, doctors and nurses. She offers friendly chit-chat to all who come her way, rearranges the photos in patients' rooms to give them something new to look at and tries to clean those rooms at times most convenient to relatives.

Contact with people is one of the important reasons that jobs yield satisfaction. So don't be afraid to enjoy contact with workmates—something that's important to all of us, but particularly important for people with uninspiring jobs. Having a laugh, sharing a little gossip and socialising after work are natural and healthy things to do. And there's room for a little harmless practical joking.

A lot of job enjoyment comes from our own attitudes and behaviour. So it's in our own interests to cultivate the attitudes conducive to greater happiness. One good rule is: don't sweat the small stuff. A lot of workers get browned off about the paperwork they're required to process, finding it hard to see what use it is. My attitude has been that, if all it takes to keep the higher-ups happy is to fill in their silly forms on time, why not? What's so hard about a form?

I can imagine cleaning supervisors being less than sympathetic to cleaners who want to chat to patients. Get on with your work! Supervisors oughtn't to be so blinkered about the wider purposes of the game, but no doubt many are. It's then a question of finding a balance between keeping your boss happy and doing your job the way you feel it ought to be done. If that balance involves a little unpaid overtime, so be it.

No one enjoys being taken advantage of, but if you work for a big corporation don't get too hung up about the huge profits they're making. Remember that, in these days of compulsory superannuation saving, Australia's big companies are increasingly owned by the workforce, including you. The big profits they're ripping out are fattening our retirement payouts.

In your dealings with bosses, beware of what the psychologists call 'negative self-fulfilling expectancies'. As you've probably noticed with children—perhaps with yourself—people have a tendency to conform to the expectations of them. Keep telling a kid how clumsy she is and she'll get worse. Assume your kid lies to you and he soon will (especially if he knows you're not very trustworthy yourself). My mother used the opposite psychology on me: she assumed I would always be scrupulously honest and I rarely disappointed her.

Bosses are just like children. The more you automatically assume they're square in their dealings with you—and let them see that confidence in them—the less likely they are to let you down. But let them see you don't trust them or don't believe what they say and you'll be proved right. Bosses have been known to issue more IOUs than they'll ever be able to honour. If so, the workers whose IOUs are most likely to be dishonoured are those who expect them to be dishonoured. It's called human nature.

According to the British human relations firm Chiumento, the top ten things workers want are: friendly and supporting colleagues, enjoyable work, a good boss or manager, good work–life balance, varied work, something worthwhile to do, work that makes a difference, being part of a successful team, having achievements recognised, and a competitive salary. By now you can see the truth in most of those.

Timothy Sharp, the clinical psychologist and founder of the Happiness Institute in Sydney—also known as Dr Happy—has his own tips for happiness at work. One is to stop doing things you hate. We often spend a lot of time doing tasks we think are essential, but are really optional. So quit doing the stuff you hate and see if anyone notices. Or delegate tasks you dread to someone who enjoys that type of work. 'One of the mistakes we make is thinking, "I don't like this, so no one will",' he says.

Another tip is to focus on the positives. Many of us have a tendency to focus on the bad things, he says, but there are few organisations that are totally terrible, and for every problem or colleague you don't like there are almost certainly good things and nice people. So be grateful and focus on the good things about your workplace, your role or your co-workers.

Get into flow

One way of getting more happiness into your job is so important it deserves a heading of its own. Flow is the discovery of Mihaly Csikszentmihalyi (pronounced chick-SENT-me-hi and literally translated as Michael St Michael of Csik, a town in

Transylvania), a professor of psychology at Claremont Graduate University in California. Mihaly identified four ways by which we can turn adversity or boredom into enjoyment: set goals, immerse yourself in the activity, pay attention to what's happening and enjoy the immediate experience. All of those things are embodied in the state of 'flow'. To be in a state of flow is to be so absorbed in what you're doing that you lose all sense of time and self. It's obviously totally focused on the intrinsic.

It's exhilarating to flow with an activity that fully engages our skills. But it's not an experience in which you feel great pleasure because you're not conscious of anything to do with yourself. It's only in retrospect that you realise how happy you were. Flow experiences boost our subsequent feelings of self-esteem, competence and wellbeing.

The central requirement for attaining a state of flow is that the task involve a challenge that's equal to our skills. If the challenge is greater than our abilities we'll be overwhelmed, whereas if it's not up to our abilities we'll be underwhelmed. We also need to find meaning in our work.

Flow is most often encountered at work, but it can also be achieved in leisure pursuits. It was through beeping volunteers for his studies on thousands of occasions to report on what they were doing and how they were feeling about it that Mihaly was struck by the relative poverty of experience in free time, the emptiness of most leisure. 'Most dimensions of experience,' he says, 'people report being more passive, irritable, sad, weak and so forth. To fill the void in consciousness, people turn on the TV or find some other way of structuring experience vicariously. These passive leisure activities take the worst edge off the threat of chaos, but leave the individual feeling weak and enervated.'

Bosses and workers

If economics is subject to fashion, management is subject to fads. I must confess I have trouble making sense of the business books I try to read, and usually don't finish. But I did get a lot out of one a few years back by two journalists on *The Economist*, John Micklethwait and Adrian Wooldridge, called *The Witch Doctors*. That book argued that management theory is not so much a coherent discipline as a battleground between two radically opposed philosophies of human nature.

At one extreme is Frederick Taylor's early 20th-century theory of 'scientific management', which is based on the idea that the average worker is a lazy dolt who's redeemed only by greed. In this scenario the job of the manager is to break down jobs into their component parts, so that even the dumbest can master them, and to design incentive systems so that even the laziest will exert himself. Apart from that, workers need to be closely supervised at all times.

At the other extreme is the 'human relations school'—also having its origins in the early 20th century—which is based on the idea that the average worker is a model human being, intelligent, creative and self-motivating. The job of the manager is to ensure that work is interesting enough to bring out the best in their employees, by devolving decisions to the shop floor, creating self-managing teams and encouraging workers to suggest improvements.

The authors' point was that, when you examine it closely, every new management fad can be put into one of these boxes or the other, and successive Breakthroughs in management theory merely oscillate between the two extremes. The battle between these opposing views has never been resolved because, presumably, the truth lies somewhere in the middle.

But the question for our purposes is whether the new science of happiness can help resolve the dispute.

What's in it for the boss?

Personally, I can't imagine why any chief executive would want to be the captain of an unhappy ship. Why does that sound attractive? I think there probably are some bosses who believe keeping their troops fearful and insecure is the best way to keep them on their toes and working hard, but I know of no hard evidence to support such a misanthropic view of working life.

I suspect, however, that the main reason so many workplaces aren't particularly desirable places to work is that bosses think worrying about their workers' job satisfaction is a luxury they have neither the time nor the money to afford. If they don't get sales or profits or the share price (or the circulation) up in a hurry, they'll be out. They may also fear that a 'satisfied' workforce may not see a need to try very hard.

And I have to tell you that, at least until relatively recently, the well-informed boss was right to be sceptical about whether attempts to raise the job satisfaction of his troops carried any benefits for the business's bottom line. Twenty-five years ago two psychologists at Iowa State University, Michelle Iaffaldano and Paul Muchinsky, conducted a meta-analysis (a study of studies) of 217 studies on the relationship between job satisfaction and job performance. They concluded the two were 'only slightly related'.

Michael Argyle's somewhat more recent summary of the evidence on job satisfaction wasn't quite so dismissive. He says some studies have found a stronger correlation between the job satisfaction and the performance of more highly skilled workers, such as managers and professionals. He says studies find only small correlations between job satisfaction and absenteeism, but this may be partly because absenteeism tends to be concentrated among a small number of workers. And absenteeism is affected by factors other than job satisfaction, such as child care. However, there's a stronger correlation between job satisfaction and labour turnover. The correlation is stronger in times of low unemployment, which is when the need to hang on to good workers is greater. Job satisfaction is as strong as wage levels as a predictor of whether workers will quit.

Business people often say that what they value is not job satisfaction so much as 'engagement' with the business's goals. This may explain the more recent research interest in 'oganis- ational citizenship behaviour'—how likely workers are to help others, make suggestions and do the right thing (such as being punctual or not wasting time) without having to be monitored. Studies have shown a stronger, two-way relationship with job satisfaction.

I think it's relevant to note that the nature of work has changed significantly in recent decades, with consequent impli- cations for the management of workers. A British study has shown that the use of advanced technology has considerably increased the skills used at all levels. We're working with more sophisticated machines, which now do almost all of the drudgery. My observation is that while computerisation has made some work more unpleasant—call centres, for instance— many more jobs have been made more highly skilled, intellectually demanding and potentially satisfying.

The workforce needs to be—and is—more highly skilled and better educated, and thus more highly paid. Work has become less physical and more cerebral, making many more of us 'symbolic analysts', as Robert Reich put it. The phenomenal growth of the services sector—which accounts for all the growth in employment over the past 20 years—has increased the requirement for workers who, because they deal directly with patients, clients or customers, need to be friendly and helpful.

All this says to me that bosses can no longer afford to be quite so cavalier about how satisfying their workers find the tasks and working conditions they're given. It suggests that their happiness is more likely to affect the firm's productivity and profits. It also suggests that work effort has become discretionary in the sense that it has become a lot harder and more expensive to monitor than it was in the days of production lines and physical output.

So although many hard-headed bosses recoil from such a touchy-feely notion as 'happiness', it's not surprising that, more recently, the happiness researchers have uncovered strong causal links running from happiness to business success.

Before we get to the psychologists, however, let's note the assessment of two economists, Bruno Frey and Alois Stutzer, in their book *Happiness and Economics*. 'In general,' they say, 'overall job satisfaction and performance are positively related. It stands to reason that dissatisfied people do not work well, impose high costs on the employers by being more often absent from the job, and change jobs more frequently than other people.

'Employees experiencing little satisfaction from their work and having low intrinsic motivation cannot be expected to engage themselves in the organisation and be creative and innovative. This is very important because, in most jobs, the employers can monitor their employees only very partially; it is therefore necessary to rely, at least partly, on the workers' intrinsic motivation. Dissatisfied employees also have little incentive to think seriously about whether the tasks they perform are sensible for the goals of the organisation they work in.'

Bruno and Alois warn, however, that having satisfied workers isn't always a blessing for a firm. Evidence suggests that, beyond a certain level, very high job satisfaction is no longer conducive to the firm's goals. The employees enjoy themselves at work, but don't necessarily do the hard work also required.

Ask a boss what qualities they look for in a prospective employee and they'll probably list intelligence, a good education, hard work, social skills, social connections, trustworthiness, reliability and ability. They probably won't add that the workers should be happy, positive and optimistic. But the Dieners are in absolutely no doubt that 'happy workers are good workers'.

In one study designed to explore the influence of happiness on success, Ed Diener and colleagues obtained data on the cheerfulness of students entering college in 1976 and then checked on their incomes in the 1990s, when the subjects were nearing middle age. Whereas the least cheerful people were earning about $50,000 a year, the most cheerful were earning about $65,000—30 per cent more. Even after allowing for other factors, such as the subjects' occupations and the start they got from their parents, the cheerfulness factor was still significant.

Could it be that a bit of positivity really translates into a more efficient, more productive employee? Research shows that both supervisors and customers think so. In one study, supervisor evaluations of workers were compared with the happiness tests the workers had completed several years earlier. The workers' degree of happiness at the earlier time predicted how well the supervisors evaluated their work.

In other studies undertaken with MBA students and

corporate employees it was found that happy students and happy workers were more effective decision-makers, received better performance evaluations from teachers and management and ended up with more pay rises.

The Dieners say happiness also translates into more creativity at work. Happy workers are better at producing fresh ideas for changing products and services, as well as suggesting clever new procedures that allow their organisations to achieve important goals. 'Creativity has long been linked to happiness because a good mood facilitates broader thinking and the more original thoughts that are fundamental to coming up with new ideas,' they say.

In summary, happy workers make more money, receive more promotions and better supervisor ratings and are better citizens at work. Why might this be? First, the Dieners say, because happy people are more sociable, and so customers, colleagues and supervisors resonate well with their warm, friendly attitudes. Second, happy people tend to have more energy and enthusiasm, and are more likely to work hard and confidently. Third, happy individuals experience fewer distractions as a result of personal problems, such as marital discord and alcohol abuse. Fourth, happy workers are inclined to be more creative than their peers and are therefore good at generating ideas and solving problems. Finally, happy workers are healthier, and therefore more likely to show up for work and be fit to work.

'The modern organisation that can create calling-oriented workers who are loyal to the company has a clear advantage over its competitors,' they conclude. Sonja Lyubomirsky seconds the motion. 'Happier people have been found to be more creative and productive,' she writes on her blog. 'They are better "organisational citizens" (going above and beyond their job duties), better negotiators and are less likely to take sick days, to quit or to suffer burnout.'

How to keep workers happy

If only half of all that were true it would still be the case that bosses who aren't concerned about the happiness and job satisfaction of their workers are leaving themselves vulnerable to their competitors. The first thing it suggests is that firms ought to select for happiness among the people they hire.

But when you want to hire the best available, that becomes a two-way street. Why would a happy and successful and thus highly desirable employee want to work for a company without a good reputation for the way it treats its staff? While an economy's recessed, a poor reputation is something firms can get away with. But when a recovery is well underway and the effects of the ageing of the population reassert themselves, the competition for good skilled workers will return. And it seems only a matter of time before a rating system of companies' records as employers is developed and made available on the internet.

I've long believed that good companies go out on the market and buy the best-performing employees (thus bidding up salaries), whereas the smartest companies concentrate on training up good performers in-house. It's better to grow your own 'calling-oriented' workers than to poach your competitors' 'career-oriented' workers.

So what do you have to do to create an environment conducive to the propagation of intrinsically motivated workers? More generally, how do you achieve a high level of job satisfaction?

The first thing for bosses to be clear on—because it's not a notion that comes naturally to the managerial class—is that pay is not the only motivator. 'The truth is, while all workers are concerned with their compensation and prefer to make more than less, healthy paycheques and robust retirement plans by themselves will not produce a happy workforce,' the Dieners say. 'Many employees, especially those in typical middle-class jobs, care about an additional thousand dollars much less than they want their work to be challenging, meaningful and collegial. Even with average pay and benefits, workers may be very happy with their jobs if the other factors are in place.'

This is particularly true of those workers who might be encouraged to see their work as a calling, of course. To be cynical about it, this is good news for a canny boss. It means there are a lot of ways to reward and encourage workers that don't cost all that much. (It's always amazed me that so many of my bosses have been so neglectful in passing a personal compliment to someone who's doing well. What could be cheaper?)

Employees' concern for non-monetary benefits is a two-edged sword, however. It makes employers who don't worry about the attractiveness of the working environment vulnerable to rival firms that do. And remember Andrew Oswald's finding from his survey of job satisfaction: *absolute* increases in pay gratify workers less than perceived anomalies in *relative* pay upset them. These days, bosses almost invariably think of rewarding the best worker in a category with more money; that can often anger and de-motivate his peers. And it encourages good workers to seek extrinsic rather than intrinsic satisfaction.

So if employers want to offer a satisfaction-inducing working environment, what must they do? The British psychologist Peter Warr has identified six factors as important to job satisfaction.

First, opportunities for personal control. This means having some discretion—autonomy—in how to tackle problems, apply skills and envisage outcomes. The Dieners say this flexibility is the key to making work feel less routine and the job more rewarding. It's so important to people that research shows workers who don't feel they have any control over their jobs suffer more health problems than workers who have some control.

Chris Popp, of the Melbourne workplace health consultancy Workplace Wellbeing, offers the pithy advice: 'Give people a say in what's going on. Given them ownership of a job and real influence in how it is done.'

Second, jobs with a variety of tasks. Many jobs are naturally varied, but highly repetitive jobs are soul-destroying. When workers work in teams, roles can be shared. On production lines, workers should be rotated through several different tasks during a day.

Third, supportive supervisors. The Dieners say good supervisors provide a balance of freedom and supervision. They are interested in continuing employee development and are eager to provide the tools and training necessary to help them do their work better. Chris Popp says: 'In a high-performing workplace the ratio of positive to negative feedback is about six to one.'

Fourth, respect and status. Jobs that afford people respect and status are likely to engender feelings of competence and pride. In the best organisations, the respect that is inherent in some high-status jobs can be extended to all jobs. Chris says: 'Foster good relationships between workers, starting from the top. Make sure everyone's views are sought and respected. Know your employees, their names and what they do. Walk through the office every day and acknowledge them.'

Fifth, good pay and fringe benefits. There's no getting around it, the Dieners say, good workplaces pay their employees a decent wage. Enough said.

Sixth, clear requirements and information on how to meet them. Workers—particularly those well down in the chain of command—become anxious and insecure when they're not sure exactly what they're required to do, how it's to be done and by when. Michael Argyle says 'role conflict'—where an individual is under different pressures from others—and 'role ambiguity' are a source of irritation, anxiety or even depression.

In thinking further about what needs to be done to achieve high job satisfaction it's worth noting Dave Myers' factors that create it. Work gives us personal identity, allows us to identify with a community, adds purpose to our lives and provides us with a sense of personal control. So there are benefits to employers in encouraging a sense of camaraderie among staff: facilitating the social club, paying for the Christmas party and, to quote Chris Popp, 'encouraging laughter and humour, but not at anyone's expense'.

Knock-off time

If, as someone has said, happiness comes from being purposefully occupied, that makes our work—paid or voluntary, out of the home or in the home—pretty important. We look to work for fulfilment, stimulation and friendship.

But that requires it to be, as the psychologists keep saying, 'meaningful' work. Meaningful work is work where the chief benefit is intrinsic to the work itself, with the monetary payment being necessary but secondary. C.S. Lewis once said: 'I am doing work which is worth doing. It would still be worth doing if nobody paid for it. But as I have no private means, and need to be fed and housed and clothed, I must be paid while I do it.'

The Dieners say the links between happiness and health, relationships and work are the foundation of a portfolio of psychological wealth. Success in these life domains tends to boost happiness. And positive emotions, in turn, tend to lead to success in these life domains.

6

HOW TO BE HAPPY

Being rich is better than being poor—if only for financial reasons.
— Woody Allen, who would make a good economist

The simple, perhaps surprising, truth is that most of us are quite happy. According to the Australian Unity Wellbeing Index—the main regular measure of happiness in Australia—the average score from many surveys over the years is about 75 out of 100. That's not too bad. It suggests that the human animal is built to be happy. But even for those individuals with scores around the average there's still room for improvement and, of course, many people fall below the average.

As we saw in Chapter 3, although about half our level of happiness is determined by the genes we inherit, that leaves plenty of scope for us to influence our own happiness by the things we do. And the psychologists who specialise in the study of what they call subjective wellbeing now know a lot about the things that do—and don't—contribute to our happiness.

Prominent among these specialists is Professor Sonja Lyubomirsky, of the University of California, Riverside. In her book *The How of Happiness*, she argues that the things we've been conditioned to believe will make us lastingly happy won't do so. 'Psychological scientists have amassed persuasive evidence that we are routinely off base about what will bring us pleasure and fulfilment, and as a result, we sometimes work to make things happen that don't actually make us happy,' she says.

Perhaps the greatest single mistake we make is imagining that changing the *circumstances* of our lives will make a big difference to our happiness. If only we had a little more money, or a better job, if only we lived in a better area, had a better house, a better spouse or better children, things would be so much . . . well, better. We're all tempted to think it, but for the most part it's wrong.

Research by Sonja and her colleagues has found that our circumstances account for as little as 10 per cent of the difference between our level of happiness and other people's. Much of our circumstances can't be changed—our age, gender, race or height, for instance—while most of the rest can be changed only with great difficulty—our education, occupation, marriage, family, health or looks. But even the stuff that can be changed with effort—our job, our house, the city we live in—is likely to make far less difference to our happiness than we imagine. There are two main reasons for this.

The first is that—as Daniel Gilbert, professor of psychology at Harvard, explains in his book *Stumbling on Happiness*—although humans are the only animal capable of imagining the future, we're not very good at it. We almost always overestimate how much happier some positive event will make us feel, while also overestimating how unhappy some negative event will make us feel. Studies have found, for instance, that gaining job tenure doesn't make academics feel nearly as happy as they imagined it would, while splitting up with a boyfriend or girlfriend doesn't make students feel nearly as bad as they imagined.

The second reason changing our circumstances does so little to affect our happiness—and a big part of the reason we're so bad at predicting how events will affect our happiness—is because of 'hedonic adaptation' or habituation, as discussed in Chapter 3. However wonderful we may find some event at first—a pay rise or promotion, a new house or new car—the thrill quickly wears off and we soon regard it as part of the status quo.

No, the more important conclusion is that it's not changing our circumstances that makes us happier, it's changing our *behaviour*. What matters most is what we *do*, but also how we think. Why? Because this is the remaining 40 per cent of the difference between our happiness and other people's that is left after taking account of the 50 per cent determined by our genes and the 10 per cent determined by our circumstances.

According to Sonja Lyubomirsky: '. . . a massive [scientific] literature reveals what kinds of attributes, thoughts and behaviours characterise the happiest people. In my laboratory and the laboratories of a few others, ways of harnessing the power of our own thoughts and behaviours—that is, our intentional activities—have been tested.'

Sonja says happiness is not out there for us to find. The reason it's not *out* there is that it's *inside* us. More than anything, happiness is a state of mind, a way of perceiving and approaching ourselves and the world we live in. The only catch is that changing the way we think and act takes effort. 'Becoming lastingly happier demands making some permanent changes that require effort and commitment every day of your life. Pursuing happiness takes work, but consider that this "happiness work" may be the most rewarding work you'll ever do.'

So now let me give you my ten principles for improving your happiness. For the most part they're drawn from the research of Sonja and many other psychologists specialising in this area, although I'll add my own thoughts and experience. Most of them won't come as a great surprise to you, but now you'll know they're backed by solid research evidence. Some of them you'll already be doing, but that's okay. It's nice to have the reinforcement, and nice to know what among all the things you're doing enjoys the scientists' imprimatur. If you're not doing most of them then the good news is you've plenty of room for improvement. But I'd start with just a few of them—the ones most apposite to your needs—rather than trying to change yourself in many ways and soon discovering it's all too hard.

1. Focus on the human, not the material

The slogan that 'people matter more than things' is one few, if any, people would disagree with. We know it's true because people—our mothers, fathers, siblings, spouses, children and grandchildren—play such a large part in our own lives. And that's not counting our extended family, friends, workmates and neighbours. If we're honest with ourselves we know we're obsessed by our family relationships—even those rellos we may have fallen out with.

We care about our relationships with people because humans are a highly social animal. In the language of a psychologist, humans are powerfully motivated by a pervasive drive to seek out and maintain strong, stable and positive interpersonal relationships. We strongly resist the breakup or dissolution of relationships and friendships, and without a sense of belongingness we suffer numerous negative consequences for our physical and mental health.

The explanation for our obsession with human relationships is clearly evolutionary. 'Human beings would not have been able to survive or reproduce without such a motivation,' Sonja says. 'Social groups hunted together, shared food and fought off common enemies. Adults who pair-bonded bore children, protected them from predators and from the elements, and raised them to maturity.'

Our evolution from such tightly knit groups explains our need to belong, to fit in and to be loved. We need to receive love and support from others, but also to give it. Try to live a life of minimal social intimacy and expect to be deeply unhappy. Indeed, you'd have to be already emotionally scarred to want such a life.

But all this just makes it more puzzling that we need reminding that 'people matter more than things'. We know it all too well, but we keep forgetting it. Too often we give material concerns priority over the maintenance of healthy relationships. Governments do it almost as a matter of course, but you and I do it more often than we should.

Why? Because, I suspect, we live in a highly material world, at a particularly materialist stage in its development. Our bigger and ever more complex world makes it harder for us to see the importance of our most elemental human relationships, while the advertising that seeks to keep the capitalist machine ever turning over and expanding manipulates our subconscious into believing that, in fact, things matter more than people. The unspoken message of advertising is that whatever's being flogged—from margarine to a Mercedes—is just the thing to make us, and our nearest and dearest, truly happy.

This is not to deny the importance of the material. We literally can't live without it. And genuine material deprivation isn't a good recipe for wellbeing. It's just a matter of getting our priorities right. Executives who works such long hours their children hardly see them may tell themselves they do it to give those kids a wonderful life of private schools and privilege. It's probably not their real reason; they're probably spoiling their kids and they probably won't end up thanking their absentee benefactor. Similarly, the second-earner who goes back to work earlier than they should because their family 'just can't make ends meet' is probably more concerned with maintaining a standard of living than with ensuring their kids don't starve.

The unit of currency for materialism is, of course, money. It's important stuff, we can't live without it, but most of us—my good self included—give it more attention than we should. In their book *Happiness*, Ed Diener and Robert Biswas-Diener seek to put money in its right place by introducing the concept of 'psychological wealth'. This covers all the resources a person needs to live a good life. Besides money, the wealth we need includes positive spirituality (the experiencing of positive emotions that link us to things larger than ourselves), a favourable outlook for the future and—saving the most important for last—supportive relationships.

On his website Ed Diener offers a shortlist of 'steps people can take to ensure they are as happy as they can be'. First on the list is 'we need good friends and family, and we may need to sacrifice to some extent to ensure we have intimate, loving relationships—people who care about us, and about whom we care deeply'.

David Myers is professor of psychology at Hope College, Michigan, author of America's best-selling introductory textbooks on psychology and social psychology, particularly nice guy and author of the book that, purchased second hand at an Easter Saturday book sale in the progress association hall of a coastal holiday village, first sparked my interest in this topic, *The Pursuit of Happiness*. Dave also gives top billing to close, supportive relationships. People supported by intimate friendships or a committed marriage are much likelier to declare themselves 'very happy', he says. 'Resolve to nurture your closest relationships: to *not* take those closest to you for granted, to display to them the sort of kindness that you display to others, to affirm them, to play together and share together.'

Sonja Lyubomirsky says the causal relationship between social relationships and happiness is clearly 'bidirectional'. This means having romantic partners and friends makes people happy, but also that happy people are more likely to acquire lovers and friends. This implies that any effort you make to improve your relationships is likely to have a big and early payoff.

One of the big problems with money as a source of happiness is adaptation—the speed with which we get used to having what we have or any increase. In one study that surveyed people for 36 years, respondents were asked how much income was needed by a family of four to 'get along'. The higher the person's income, the more they estimated such a family would need. But get this: the estimate people gave for how much was needed to get by increased almost exactly in line with the respondents' actual income. As our income increases our aspirations quickly adjust to fit and we soon feel no better off.

By contrast, studies show we don't have nearly the same degree of adaptation to marriage, relationships and friendships. Why not? Because we're such social animals, because relations with others are so integral to our emotional and physical wellbeing. One of the most important functions of a social bond is the provision of support at times of stress, distress and trauma. Such support can be practical, emotional or informational.

Sonja's book elaborates on David Myers' suggestions on what we can do to nurture our relationships. For marriages, she recommends committing to extra time each week with your partner, perhaps starting with one hour and working your way up. Express admiration, appreciation and affection. One of the key conclusions of two decades of research on marriages is that happy relationships are characterised by a ratio of positive to negative comments of five to one.

Another strategy involves taking delight in your partner's, family members' or friends' successes and good fortune. 'Social psychologists have shown that what distinguishes good and poor relationships is not how the partners respond to each other's disappointments and reversals, but how they respond to *good* news,' Sonja says.

Turning to friendships, Sonja and her colleagues asked 500 university students what strategies they used to increase their happiness. Top of their list was 'social affiliation'—hanging around with friends, helping others—and this activity had the strongest correlation with the students' actual happiness.

Studies have found that, relative to married people, singles are closer to their friends and have more frequent contact with them. Lifelong single older women tend to have close to a dozen devoted decades-long friends. According to a British study quoted by the *Guardian* newspaper, the ideal number of friends—presumably, whether or not you're married—is ten. You have a 40 per cent chance of being happy if you have five friends or fewer, rising to 50 per cent if you have up to ten, while any more than that increases your chances only to 55 per cent. (Don't believe it if you don't want to.)

2. Work on making other people happy, not yourself

There's a trick to happiness and it's such an important principle I considered listing it first: it can't be sought directly. Like various other goals in life, if it's to be approached successfully it must be approached indirectly. When I was growing up I imagined I'd get married when I reached 21. When, after I'd turned 21, nothing had happened I got quite anxious about it, especially as none of the women I liked were interested. I guess my impatience put them off. Eventually, however, I calmed down and just got on with enjoying women's company. And then, not surprisingly, nature took its course and marriage followed.

If you're forever asking yourself, 'Am I happy? Am I happy?', the answer will be no. The watched pot never boils. Acting directly to make yourself feel happy leads you to hedonistic self-indulgence, which may bring pleasure, but only fleetingly. If you focus on the wellbeing of others, however, every so often you wake up and realise that, though you hadn't noticed, you are happy.

Samuel Levenson observed that 'happiness is a by-product; you cannot pursue it by itself'. John Stuart Mill never wavered in his conviction that happiness was the purpose of life, but also believed that those who achieved it 'have their minds fixed on some other object', such as the wellbeing of others or some art or pursuit. Aldous Huxley said, 'happiness is like coke—something you get as a by-product in the process of making something else'.

And someone reviewing Mike Leigh's film *Happy-Go-Lucky* observed: 'The happiest people in the world, according to one theory, barely know they're happy. They're too busy. Their commitment to satisfying love and fulfilling work leaves them no time for self-pity, regret, fears of the future or any other source of unhappiness.'

The principle of indirectness is so well established there's even a fancy name for it: the 'teleological paradox'—you can't achieve some objective by pursuing it directly. I can't find that the psychologists have done many studies to confirm this truth, but in David Myers' book he quotes an experiment by Bernard Rimland.

Rimland asked 216 students to list the initials of the ten people they knew best, yielding a grand list of some 2000 people. He then asked them to indicate whether each person seemed happy or not. Finally, he asked them to go over each name again, indicating if the person seemed selfish (devoted mostly to his or her own welfare) or unselfish (willing to be inconvenienced for others). The striking result: 70 per cent of those judged unselfish seemed happy; 95 per cent of those judged selfish seemed *un*happy.

What a paradox, said the surprised Rimland: 'Selfish people are, by definition, those whose activities are devoted to *bringing themselves happiness.* Yet, at least as judged by others, these selfish people are far *less* likely to be happy than those whose efforts are devoted to making others happy.'

Why this correlation between selfless, altruistic living and happiness, Dave asks. 'Certainly one reason . . . is that happiness makes people less self-focused and more altruistic. But it works the other way around, too. Doing good makes us feel good. Altruism enhances our self-esteem. It gets our eyes off ourselves, makes us less self-preoccupied and gets us closer to the unself-consciousness that characterises the flow state.'

3. Seek benefits that are intrinsic, not instrumental

Do things for their own sake, not because of the income or status you hope they will bring you. This is particularly true of work. Life's too short to spend 40 hours-plus a week doing something you hate, just because the money's better. As the Defence Forces recruitment ad says, find a job you love and you'll never have to work again. It's better to forget the money and try to get into a virtuous circle: you like the work because you're good at it and you're good at it because you like it. With any luck, pay rises follow.

Robert Frank, a professor of economics at Cornell University, must be a smart chap because he agrees with me. 'Those who focus most consciously and intensively on material success also tend to experience low levels of measured happiness', he wrote in *The New York Times*. 'A far more promising strategy, according to the happiness literature, is to seek work you love. Those who find such a calling typically become deeply engaged in their professional lives. And engagement, in turn, leads to expertise, which in some fields, at least, leads to wealth. Finding work that you value for its own sake is thus not only a promising path to happiness, it may also increase your chances of becoming rich. But even if not, it will improve your odds of becoming an interesting person, someone who is attractive to both friends and potential mates alike.'

Simon Tupman says, 'the challenge in life is to be able to put a check mark in all of the three circles: to use their professional skills to the maximum; to do something that has purpose; and to do something they feel passionate about'.

Education's much the same story. It's more enjoyable and beneficial if you can find an interest in the subject for its own sake rather than seeing it as no more than a path to a good job. Uni lecturer mates tell me that, whenever they stray into some related area of interest, their students are always demanding, 'Is this examinable?' If it's not, they don't want to know. Not a smart attitude.

Of course, some of us may not be free to leave the work we're doing or the courses we've enrolled in, and even in our dream job there'll be aspects of it we don't enjoy, not to mention all the chores we can't avoid around the home. This is where it's handy to help things along with a bit of positive thinking. I once noted down a thought that the greatest gift is the ability to enjoy doing what you're obliged to do anyway.

James Barrie wrote that the secret of happiness is not in doing what you like, but in liking what you have to do. And Disney's version of *Mary Poppins* had the right idea:

> In every job that must be done
> There is an element of fun;
> You find the fun, and—*snap*—
> The job's a game!

4. Strive for balance

I can't find any of the psychologists advocating or studying this principle, but it seems obviously sensible to me. Maybe it's the accountant in me. We have an increasing tendency to go overboard in one direction or the other, but contrast is enjoyable—a change is as good as a holiday—and a balanced life is likely to be more satisfying.

Work is good, a career is good, family is good and leisure is good. It's just a question of getting a decent balance between them. Work hard and play hard isn't a bad motto—though that may be a bit exhausting for workers with young families. It's a mistake to dream of never having to work. If you never work, you never get a holiday. Part of the trick to achieving a satisfactory balance between different aspects of your life is to make sure you don't get confused between means and ends.

Extremists—workaholic bosses, in particular—are always trying to make us feel guilty about too many public holidays, four weeks' annual leave and not wanting to work at weekends. Nonsense. What's the point of being comfortably well off materially—as most of us are (if you doubt that, you've got a problem)—if we can't enjoy our prosperity? And enjoying it takes time. As does maintaining a good relationship with our kids. The key to getting more balance into your life is to be less wedded to working long hours to make the money to buy the stuff to keep up with your neighbours. Be less greedy about stuff, but also about things to do.

When I had a young family but wanted to spend a fair bit of time at work, I decided to reduce my life to just two elements: work and family. When I wasn't at work I'd be at home, and when I wasn't at home I'd be at work. Why do we feel pushed for time even at the weekend? Because we have so many options, such a wide choice of things to do. Trying to fit in too many of them is a form of greed—which leaves us feeling unsatisfied and unrefreshed.

5. Cultivate optimism

Optimism is a major focus of study for happiness researchers and the positive psychology movement. The good news is that the great majority of us are optimists, which does much to explain why most people are quite happy. The research shows that happy people tend to be optimists and optimists tend to be happy people. In other words, being happy makes you optimistic and being optimistic makes you happy.

It seems likely that our optimistic or pessimistic temperament is inherited. But the Dieners say optimism isn't simply a matter of inborn temperament, but is also a skill that can be learnt by recognising unhelpful thinking strategies and replacing them with more positive ones.

What exactly is an optimist? It's someone who retains a sense of hope for the future and who interprets life events in a positive way. It's someone who always sees the glass as half full, of course, but there's more to it. Say some negative or unpleasant event has occurred; say, you tried to sell your car but failed. An optimist is someone who attributes that failure to causes that are external ('it's the recession'), transient ('the market won't be down for long') or specific ('people in my neighbourhood don't go for that model'), as opposed to causes that are internal, long lasting and pervasive ('I've never been good at selling things').

The point of all this is that it's not what happens to us that matters, so much as how we interpret what happens to us. Experiments by Sonja Lyubomirsky show that happy people naturally reinterpret events so as to preserve their self-esteem. The Dieners offer a list of common thinking pitfalls that leave people feeling bad:

- 'awfulising', in which people exaggerate how negative an event or a person is. A wife, for instance, might think of her husband, 'He's totally inconsiderate because he rarely does the dishes';

- distress intolerance, in which people underestimate their ability to recover from a painful event. Many events are pretty terrible—divorce, for instance—but we do recover from them;
- learnt helplessness, in which people simply give up because they feel they're powerless to change their circumstances. 'Why bother?' is the telltale sign;
- perfectionism, in which people strive to be faultless rather than just successful. Perfectionists often pay more attention to the small details that went wrong than to the big picture of everything that went right;
- negative self-fulfilling expectations, in which you draw negative responses from others by communicating that you expect a negative reaction. Oh yes. I've seen a lot of that;
- rejection goggles, which cause people to see rejections everywhere, even in normal encounters. And even the most minor rejection can be seen as a major slight.

The answer to such debilitating ways of thinking is to learn to think more positively. The Dieners' solution is to encourage sufferers to 'take AIM at happiness', where A stands for attention (looking for the good things that happen or the good aspects of mixed events), I stands for interpretation (thinking of neutral events as positive and seeing adverse events as opportunities for growth) and M for memories (regularly recalling and recounting all the good things that have happened to us).

Sonja advances three main reasons why optimistic thinking boosts happiness. First, if you're optimistic about the future—for example, you're confident you'll be able to achieve your lifetime goals—you'll put effort into achieving those goals. So optimistic thoughts can be self-fulfilling. What's more, an optimistic outlook will carry you through the inevitable obstacles to your goals. Optimists have more goals, are more motivated and don't give up easily, which helps explain why they tend to be more successful—and thus happier.

Second, optimistic thinking enhances happiness by prompting us to engage in active and effective coping. There's much evidence that optimists routinely maintain relatively high levels of wellbeing and mental health during times of stress. For instance, optimistic women are less likely to become depressed following childbirth. Even at the worst of times, such as after receiving a grave health diagnosis, they don't deny the situation but instead are likely to accept the reality of their condition and make efforts to make the best of it and even grow from it.

Third, and not surprisingly, optimistic thinking promotes positive moods, vitality and high morale. Optimists are more likely to report a sense of mastery and high self-regard and less likely to experience depression and anxiety. It feels good to believe your prospects are bright. If you have something to look forward to you'll feel energised, motivated and enthusiastic. You'll feel good about yourself and feel able to control your destiny. And guess what—you'll be better liked by others. The Dieners say optimists tend to be cheerful and frequent smilers, which makes people like them.

It's worth noting that optimism is good for the economy. Indeed, capitalist economies advance on the backs of optimists. Business people tend to be more optimistic than average. Although of late the global economy has suffered from an excess of risk-taking, especially by the financial markets, as a more general proposition we need businesses willing to take risks with new inventions, new products and new ways of doing things.

Were our business people not the optimists they are, our material standard of living wouldn't be as high as it is.

Of course, a lot of business people—including a lot of those who launch themselves in a small business—end up having been more optimistic about their chances of making a motza than was justified. And looking at optimists more generally, it's clear that their assessments aren't always realistic. Even so—and I trust this is more than just the optimist in me speaking—I'd much rather live in a world of undue optimism than the alternative. For the most part, you and I gain more than we lose from the optimism of others.

But let's be clear. The psychologists are talking about optimism within reason. They're not encouraging Pollyanna-ism, being in denial, or refusing to face up to your problems. They're just saying that attacking your problems with an optimistic frame of mind will get you further.

The last helpful hint is somewhat controversial among psychologists, but it makes sense to me because I've done it. When I first became a journalist I had a great problem with shyness. I used to hate having to phone people I didn't know—something a reporter has to do many times a day. These days, however, my colleagues react with disbelief when I confess to being shy. And perhaps these days—and in a work context—I'm not. But if so, it's because I've been faking confidence for so long it has become part of me.

Dave Myers' advice is, act happy. 'We can sometimes act ourselves into a frame of mind. Manipulated into a smiling expression, people feel better. So put on a happy face. Talk *as if* you feel positive self-esteem, are optimistic and are outgoing. Going through the motions can trigger the emotions,' he says.

6. Practise contentment

The distinguished economist Paul Samuelson—not just the author of the longest running introductory economics textbook but a Nobel Prize winner—once devised the formula 'happiness equals consumption divided by desire'. Or, to put it another way, happiness is what you have over want you want. If what you want exceeds what you have you're below par, whereas if what you want is no greater than what you have you're doing fine. And if what you want is less than what you have, you're rich.

For many of us, our desire—our 'aspirations', as politicians say—exceeds our consumption. Surveys invariably show a high proportion of people agreeing that they'd be happy if only their income was 'just a little higher'. Trouble is, they go on thinking this no matter how much their incomes rise. In a capitalist economy we're encouraged to think just that. Business people, economists and politicians of all persuasions regard the economic growth that leads to rising material standards of living almost as the government's raison d'être. Advertising encourages us to buy more and politicians speak approvingly of the 'aspirational voter'.

When our aspirations exceed our means, only one solution occurs to us: we must work harder or strive for a pay rise or promotion. This wouldn't be a bad strategy if it weren't for the fact that—as the capitalism system requires—our aspirations don't stand still. Chase your aspirations and you find yourself on what the psychologists call the 'hedonic treadmill'—running and running without ever getting anywhere.

Perhaps it's time more of us tried the alternative strategy of cutting back our aspirations to match our means. They say success is getting what you want, happiness is appreciating what you have. And David Myers says happiness seems less a matter of getting what you want than of wanting what you've got.

Easier said than done, of course, but the key to reducing our desire for more is to stop trying to keep up with the Joneses. So their car is newer and flasher than ours—so what? It's part of our evolutionary make-up as highly social animals to want to fit in, to attain the highest status we can within the troop and to advertise it to the world. But since everyone else is also competing for status, it's an ever-more expensive game that's very hard to win. The more we can train ourselves not to care, the happier we'll be. We should worry about how people feel—that is, be considerate—but not about what they think of us. If you must compare your material score with others', compare down, not up.

In advocating the practice of contentment, however, a qualification is in order: we should be more content with our own lot, of course, not the lot of the underprivileged. Happy shouldn't mean smug.

7. Make habits of gratitude, kindness and giving

It may sound like Sunday school, but hard-boiled, evidence-driven psychologists are always urging us to express gratitude, show kindness and dig deep. The Dieners make no bones about referring to love, gratitude and compassion as 'spiritual emotions'. According to research by the psychologist Robert Emmons, when people feel grateful they not only focus on the positive aspects of their lives but also on how others have helped them, and thus the emotion of gratitude fosters a desire to reciprocate and help others. Not surprisingly, people who practise gratefulness tend to be happier.

Gratitude is more than just saying thank you. Emmons defines it as 'a felt sense of wonder, thankfulness and appreciation for life'. So here we have scientists urging us to count our blessings.

Name them one by one, in fact. Martin Seligman says his practice is 'to begin and end each day with thanks for whatever is going on in my life. Saying "I am grateful" for all that I have, all the people in my life and the opportunity to make a difference constantly reinforces the understanding that I have much to be grateful for in my life.'

Turning to kindness, its relevance is that it involves acts of kindness towards people—with many of whom we have relationships—and people and happiness are closely related. Sonja Lyubomirsky lists any number of reasons why helping brings happiness. Being kind and generous leads you to perceive others more positively and charitably, and fosters a heightened sense of interdependence and co-operation in your community.

Doing acts of kindness often relieves guilt, distress or discomfort over others' difficulties and sufferings, and encourages a sense of awareness and appreciation for your own good fortune. Providing assistance or comfort to other people can distract you from your own troubles as it shifts the focus from you to somebody else.

A considerable benefit of kindness is its effect on self-perception. You may begin to see yourself as an altruistic and compassionate person, which can promote a sense of confidence, optimism and usefulness. Finally, kindness can set off a cascade of positive social consequences. Helping others leads people to like you, appreciate you and offer gratitude. It may also lead people to reciprocate in *your* time of need. Helping others can satisfy a basic human need for connection with others, winning you smiles, thankfulness and valued friendship.

Not surprisingly, giving also gets a good wrap. Helen Keller said the simplest way to be happy is to do good. And recent research confirms the biblical assurance that it's better to give than receive. That goes for money and for practical assistance.

One study found that elderly individuals who gave little emotional or practical support to others were more than twice as likely to die during the five years the researcher followed them compared to people who gave to others.

8. Be active

Despite all the goodie-goodie talk, happiness isn't for wusses or couch potatoes. Happy people tend to be active, not passive. One of the most mistaken ideas about the pursuit of happiness is that it leads to passivity and the abandonment of ambition. Happy people have a purpose in life. They set themselves goals and achieve them. They strive—not for just personal advancement, but to make the world a better place in some small way.

Sonja Lyubomirsky says that if we observe genuinely happy people we find they don't just sit around being contented. 'They make things happen. They pursue new understandings, seek new achievements and control their thoughts and feelings.' Aristotle said happiness is a state of activity, while any number of people have made the point that happiness is a direction, not a place, that it's about the journey rather than the destination.

What kind of activities should we choose? Those that fit our needs and personalities. To reduce the effect of adaptation—getting less enjoyment out of activities because we've become used to them—we should vary their content and change their timing. Leisure pursuits should be active rather than passive. Watching television and playing video games have no correlation with happiness, whereas reading a book scores better because we have to imagine our own pictures. Playing a sport badly always beats watching the professionals.

But let's up the tempo and move from mere activity to the pursuit of goals. Sonja warns against chasing goals that have been sold to us by the larger culture: Make money! Own your own home! Look great! These materialist urgings tend to mask the pursuits more likely to deliver lasting happiness.

Sonja lists no fewer than six ways in which the pursuit of goals adds to our happiness. Committed goal pursuit provides us with a sense of purpose and a feeling of control over our lives. (Gordon Livingston, the psychiatrist author of *Too Soon Old, Too Late Smart*, says the three components of happiness are someone to love, something to look forward to and something to do.)

Having meaningful goals bolsters our self-esteem, stimulating us to feel confident and efficacious. And the accomplishment of every sub-goal gives us an emotional boost and motivates us to continue striving. Pursuing goals adds structure and meaning to our lives—something that can be particularly important to people whose families have grown up and who've retired from daily employment.

Being committed to our goals helps us learn to master our use of time: to identify higher order goals, subdivide them into smaller steps or sub-goals and develop a schedule to accomplish them. Should we continue striving towards our goals during times of personal crisis? Research suggests that not only is it possible, but commitment to goals during such periods may help us cope better with problems. (I'm a great believer in work therapy as a treatment for bereavement and breakups.)

Finally, the pursuit of goals often involves engagement with other people—teachers, clients, colleagues, partners—and such social connections are happiness-inducing in themselves.

What goals should we pursue? Those that are intrinsic (goals we value for themselves, not as mere means to an end), authentic (goals we choose for ourselves, not ones chosen by our parents or a desire to keep up with the neighbours), approach-oriented (goals that take us towards a desirable outcome, not away from something we want to avoid), harmonious (goals that don't clash with our other goals), flexible and appropriate (the right tasks at the right time), and activity-based (goals that involve doing things rather than just changing our circumstances).

9. Live in the present

Another aspect of seeking the intrinsic is to train yourself to enjoy the moment. Sonja Lyubomirsky describes a *New Yorker* cartoon that has three panels. In the first a man is sitting at his desk and daydreaming about playing golf. In the second panel the same man is playing golf while fantasising about sex. In the third he's in bed with a woman while thinking about work. Some of us spend our lives looking forward to what's next while failing to enjoy what's now. It's not smart. Pause to remind yourself that you're happy at this very moment. Psychologists call it 'savouring' and it's a good idea.

Perhaps the best demonstration of the benefits of living in the present is achieving 'flow', the term coined by American psychologist Mihaly Csikszentmihalyi to describe the state we're in when we're so absorbed in what we're doing we lose consciousness of self and time. Again, you realise you were happy only in retrospect. Flow can be experienced at work, but also in leisure activities—gardening, craft work and even socialising.

10. Get back to nature

Humans switched from hunting and gathering to farming just 10,000 years ago. In that blink of an eye, human civilisation and sophistication has progressed far further than our evolution as a species can possibly match. The result is mismatch between our bodies and our technology that can lead to malfunctions. For instance, we've applied our technology to improving our food supply on the one hand and taking the physical effort out of work on the other. Result: an obesity epidemic.

We're happier if we do more to accommodate our unevolved bodies. I've found the best artificial prop to happiness is exercise—because it's not artificial. Like many, I've become addicted to the endorphin rush. One study asked people what strategies they used to make themselves feel better, increase their energy levels and reduce tension, and also which strategies they found most effective. Exercise was rated the most effective on all three counts, coming ahead of listening to music and social interaction (which wasn't necessarily good for making people more energetic). Strategies such as pep talks and distractions (such as shopping, reading, doing chores or pursuing hobbies) worked well for some objectives but not others. Watching television, eating and drinking coffee rated poorly.

Why does exercise make you happier? Sonja Lyubomirsky says getting exercise boosts your self-esteem and gives you a sense of mastery. It offers the potential for getting into 'flow', as well as distracting us from whatever happens to be worrying us. It's a time out from your stressful day, with positive spillover effects for hours afterwards. And when performed along with others, physical activities provide opportunities for social contact.

The feel-good consequences of exercise are probably physiological in origin. Exercise has been shown to elevate serotonin levels in the brain—similar to the effects of Prozac—although, surprisingly, Sonja says there isn't a great deal of support for the theories that vigorous physical activity elevates endorphins and induces opioids, leading to 'runners' high'. Keep looking, I say.

There's been a flood of research corroborating the many benefits of physical activity for health and wellbeing. It reduces anxiety and stress, protects us from chronic illnesses such as heart disease and some cancers, and reduces the risk of others like diabetes, colon cancer and high blood pressure, it builds bones, muscles and joints, improves quality of life, improves sleep, protects against cognitive impairments as we age and helps control weight.

Exercise is such a powerful elixir it even reduces depression. In one famous study a number of sufferers from clinical depression were divided into three groups. The first group did four months of aerobic exercise, the second group took the anti-depressant Zoloft for four months and the third group did both. It turned out that exercise was just as effective in lifting depression as the drug was, and doing both gave no extra advantage. Six months after the study ended, those who had taken the drug were more likely to have relapsed than those who did exercise.

Moving on in our back-to-nature kick there are the benefits of getting adequate sleep. I spent most of my life trying to raise my personal efficiency by minimising the time wasted in sleep. Now, having read a bit about the topic, I'm trying to raise my efficiency by making sure I get all the sleep I need. Sonja says, no matter how active, vigorous and successful we are during our waking hours, if we don't get an adequate amount of sleep we'll suffer in terms of our moods, energy, alertness, longevity and health. She quotes a prominent sleep researcher who argues that if people got just one more hour of sleep each night our 'sleep-sick' Western society would be much happier and healthier.

Now there's some research—not as much as I'd like to have been able to find—suggesting our mental health requires regular contact with grass and trees. John Zelenski, a psychologist at Canada's Carleton University, has found that people who feel connected to nature also have a sense of purpose in life and more self-acceptance. Both qualities contribute to happiness.

Not surprisingly, nature-related people spend more time outdoors. But they're also more agreeable, conscientious and open to experience. And get this: those who identified themselves as environmentalists or vegetarians rated the same as those who enjoyed hunting and fishing.

But do people love nature because they're happy, or are they happy because they love nature? Zelenski suspects both are true, but at this point he can't prove it. Keep working on it, I say.

PART TWO
MACRO HAPPINESS

7

WHAT'S WRONG WITH ECONOMICS

> An economist is a man who thinks his wife is the only
> irrational person in the economy.
> — Ross Gittins

When I was 26 I defected from accounting to economics. Since my later years at school my great ambition had been to become a chartered accountant. But by the time I'd finally achieved that exalted status I'd realised I didn't believe that what accountants did was either very interesting or very important. I drifted into general journalism, where I was soon invited to apply my commercial qualifications and experience to reporting and writing about economics. It wasn't long before I realised I had absolutely no doubt that what economists did was both interesting and important.

I've spent the past 36 years learning all I could about economics and the way economies work, and passing what I've learnt on to my readers. I've loved every moment of it and, more to the point, I've considered it a socially useful way to spend my life. And though most of this chapter is devoted to elucidating the weaknesses of economics as it is practised by too many economists, there's something I want to make crystal clear from the outset.

I believe in the value of economics and the valuable contribution economists make to society. Our considerable material prosperity—the lives of comfort, awareness and good health almost all of us in the developed countries enjoy—is owed to the market economy we live in and the never-ending technological advance it fosters. Economists are the mechanics of the market economy, studying how it works and advising the community on what needs to be done to keep it in good working order. Without that advice our material standard of living would be a lot lower. And it's by copying the well-managed economies of the rich world that the people of the poor world are now having so much success in raising their own material living standards.

At the micro level, economists have seen their role as to advise the community on ways to overcome the problem of scarcity—the conflict that arises because our wants are infinite but our resources are finite. They advise the community on ways to allocate resources more efficiently so they go further in satisfying our material wants. From scarcity comes 'opportunity cost': anything you decide to do has a cost, which is the thing you can no longer do because a dollar (or an hour of labour, or a bunch of raw materials) can only be spent once.

Opportunity cost is a pathetically simple concept, but one people are always forgetting. So it's the role of economists to keep banging on about it: choose your spending carefully because you'll be cutting off a lot of options. Were resources infinite, there'd be no need for efficiency. Since resources aren't infinite, we need to use them efficiently unless we enjoy being poor.

A lot of the people who are disdainful or dismissive of

economics don't understand it and probably don't want to. They profess to have a soul above money but, in my experience, they fight pretty hard whenever their source of money is under threat. I have no sympathy for them. Their supposed high ideals are really a refusal to accept that opportunity cost—also known by economists as the 'budget constraint'—applies to them. 'As a doctor, I must be unfettered in exercising my professional judgement in the best interests of my patient; I can't have bean counters limiting my freedom.' This is arrogance, not virtue. It's saying the taxpayer should write me an open cheque and if there's a limit on how much tax the public is prepared to pay (because of the opportunity cost of losing your income in taxes) the constraints should apply to people who aren't as important as I am. Don't bother me with the details.

I *believe* in the pursuit of efficiency. Very often, those who speak so contemptuously of efficiency are motivated by simple self-interest (though sometimes they're complaining about false economy in the name of efficiency). As we'll see, I don't believe in efficiency above all else. But efficiency should be the goal unless we've got a good enough reason to depart from it. Now we're clear on that we can proceed.

Conventional economics has lost its way. It's supposed to be about maximising happiness but it no longer is. Of course, economists wouldn't use a namby-pamby word like 'happiness'. They prefer to say 'utility'—sometimes translated as satisfaction—but it means essentially the same thing. In practice, however, utility has been redefined to mean consumption, which explains economists' obsession with promoting economic growth. The more the economy's production of goods and services grows the more goods and services we can consume, thus maximising our utility—supposedly.

How did happiness transmogrify into consumption? The big step occurred in the 1930s when economists decided that, though utility was something that couldn't be measured, this didn't matter because it could be measured indirectly by looking at what people bought. Assuming people bought what they wanted to buy, looking at their consumption would reveal their preferences. From there it was just a short step to economists becoming the great facilitators and advocators of economic growth—the high priests in the temple of Mammon.

Just a few problems. The goods and services people buy may reveal only some of their preferences. What about their preferences for non-material things—is it okay to ignore them? To take just one example, what about leisure? The economists' model correctly says we derive much utility from leisure, but the logical shortcut of 'revealed preference' means economists keep forgetting this. In any case, how do economists *know* the things we buy always accurately reflect our preferences? Do we never regret the choices we make? Are we never conned into buying things by slick marketing and advertising? And are economists still sure utility can't be measured?

Model blindness—a common affliction

These questions point to a deeper problem with economics: it's too narrow, in more ways than one. It's narrow in the sense that it's concerned with only one aspect of our lives: the material, meaning it has nothing to say about the social or the spiritual. Economists specialise in studying the production and consumption of the goods and services all of us need to live our lives. Even more narrow, they focus on those aspects of life that can be traded in the marketplace. They tend to ignore all factors not reflected in market prices and all factors that can't easily be measured in dollars. So, among a hundred examples that could be quoted, economics gives little consideration to such desirable 'goods' as love, mental challenge and the absence of stress.

This narrow focus wouldn't be so bad if so many economists—and so many fellow travellers who've incorporated conventional, neoclassical economics into their political philosophy—didn't keep forgetting what they have done. By definition, and perforce, all models of the way the world—or a bit of it—works seek to overcome the complexity of the real world by excluding those factors not judged to be germane to the purpose at hand and focusing in on those judged to be highly pertinent. As an unfortunate consequence, all professions suffer from what I call 'model blindness'—a tendency to underrate the importance of all those factors excluded from their model.

When the only tool you have is a hammer, every problem looks like a nail. Doctors have a tendency to see all problems as medical; lawyers tend to see all problems as legal. But no profession suffers from model blindness more than economics. Economists rarely warn people how narrow their perspective is and regularly push economic growth as the solution to every problem you care to name, while denying that economic growth could ever itself be a problem. Without quite realising it, they or their followers often urge us to take non-economic ends and use them as means to achieve the economic end. Cut back the number of public holidays, for instance, and we could be richer. But since we're already pretty comfortable, why can't we afford the little extra leisure public holidays provide?

But economics is also narrow in a different sense. It pretty much set its still-dominant, neoclassical model and associated assumptions in concrete in the mid-19th century and has failed to take account of subsequent advances in other sciences, particularly psychology, evolutionary biology, neuroscience and ecology. Its academics either haven't noticed these developments or don't much care about them.

At the academic level mainstream economics has become terribly inward-looking, losing interest in real-world problems while, ironically, trying to make itself more scientific—'rigorous'—by expressing analysis in mathematical equations rather than words or even diagrams. This does much to explain economists' failure to foresee the global financial crisis.

It also explains why only a relative handful of economists take much interest in the new science of happiness and its claim at last to be able to measure utility directly by means of surveys. As we saw in Chapter I, these measurements are far from perfect—but neither are many of the estimates economists happily plug into their models. This discovery by psychologists offers economists an opportunity to greatly improve their understanding of utility. And by measuring it directly they could avoid many of the drawbacks of relying on people's supposed 'revealed preference'.

More fundamentally, advances in psychology reveal how far off course are economists' conventional assumptions about the way people—'economic actors'—behave. Because it got established well before psychology had made much headway, economics is built on a particularly unrealistic model of human behaviour. Perhaps the most foundational assumption on which the whole edifice of neoclassical economics stands is the assumption that people—whether as consumers, workers, investors or business owners—are 'rational'. That is, they're invariably carefully calculating and self-interested in the decisions they make, which they always make as an individual, quite uninfluenced by the behaviour of those around them.

As one economist critic has put it, economics assumes we're all 'emotionless geniuses'. Two exponents of behavioural economics, Richard Thaler and Cass Sunstein, write in their book *Nudge* that 'if you look at economics textbooks you will learn that Homo economicus [the person who inhabits the economists' model] can think like Albert Einstein, store as much memory as IBM's Big Blue and exercise the willpower of Mahatma Gandhi'.

Rational we are not

The truth, however, as revealed by extensive psychological research, is that though humans are capable of making carefully reasoned decisions on occasion, more usually our decisions are instinctive, intuitive and emotional. As Michael Shermer wrote in *The Mind of the Market*, 'it turns out that we are remarkably irrational creatures, driven as much (if not more) by deep and unconscious emotions that evolved over the eons as we are by logic and conscious reason developed in the modern world'.

Because so many of our decisions are made so instantaneously, by the same primitive part of our brains that drives the fight-or-flight response, it's likely that often we don't actually know *why* we decided to do what we did. As we saw in Chapter 2, in a famous experiment a man who'd had the link between the two sides of his brain severed was shown a sign that commanded him to 'wave', but in such a way that the sign was visible only to the non-verbal, non-reasoning right side of his brain. He waved. Asked why he'd waved, he replied: 'I thought I saw a friend, so I waved.' The verbal, left side of his brain didn't know why he'd waved, but was adept at making up plausible explanations for his behaviour after the fact.

All the information that would be needed for us to make the carefully calculated decisions that the economists' model assumes is simply not available. But even if it were, our brains just don't have the neural processing power to carefully weigh all the options before we make the many hundreds of decisions we make each day. Rather, for those decisions we do consider we use a range of mental rules of thumb known as 'heuristics'. We rely on these mental shortcuts because, most of the time, and over the ages, they give us the right answers. In some circumstances, however, they let us down—which is why psychologists believe we are *'predictably* irrational'.

It's a mistake to imagine—as economists implicitly do—that humans' emotional nature is a sign of mental weakness, something to be regretted and overcome if possible. For a start, it's our emotions that make us human; to wish to be unemotional is to wish to be a robot. For another thing, the motivating factor behind our desire to be strictly rational in our decision-making would be to achieve our goals more effectively. But it turns out that without emotions we have no motivations, no goals. In another famous study, subjects whose brains had suffered physical damage which blocked off their emotions were found to be highly logical but completely indecisive. They endlessly evaluated the advantages and disadvantages of choices, but could never decide what to do because they lacked the desire to pursue either course. As Jonathan Haidt, a psychologist at the University of Virginia, explains in *The Happiness Hypothesis*, reason and emotion must both work together to create intelligent behaviour, but emotion does most of the work.

Although we're often quite selfish in our decisions we're not invariably self-interested, as the economists' model assumes, being perfectly capable of altruistic acts, such as tipping in restaurants we don't expect to revisit or making anonymous gifts to charity. Michael Shermer says, 'science shows that in addition to being selfish, competitive and greedy, we also harbour a great capacity for altruism, co-operation and charity'.

Similarly, we're not the rugged individualists the economists assume. We're highly social animals, at once anxious to fit in with our group and jealous of our status within the group. The social researcher Hugh Mackay says, 'the urge to belong is deeply rooted in us'. We care greatly about what other people think, including what they think of us. Our 'preferences', as economists call our likes and dislikes, aren't permanently fixed, as it suits them to assume, but are forever changing in line with our changing moods and the changing fashions within our peer group.

The fact that humans aren't the rational calculators economists assume them to be has many implications, starting with our ability to derive utility from our actions. As Bruno Frey explains in *Happiness: A Revolution in Economics*, economists assume that the utility we expect from a certain purchase or action will always equal the utility we actually experience but, in fact, we're often quite bad at predicting our utility. We tend to overestimate the pleasure we'll gain from desirable events and overestimate the pain we'll experience from undesirable events.

The problem is that, as we saw in Chapter 4, we habitually underestimate the speed with which we adapt to new developments, whether good or bad. Another problem is that, when deciding between alternatives, we tend to be more conscious of their extrinsic attributes than their intrinsic attributes. Why? Because the extrinsic is more 'salient', as psychologists say—more noticeable, more memorable. It's just a pity that the intrinsic is almost always more satisfying than the extrinsic. Doing things for their own sake is more satisfying than doing things because of the benefits they lead to.

We tend to overestimate the utility we'll derive from having a higher income in the future, but underestimate the utility to be gained from non-material aspects of life such as friendship and social relations—which helps explain why so many of us don't do as much as we could to enjoy and maintain our relationships.

It also makes economists' preoccupation with money all the more misguided. And it shows that economists fall for the same error as the rest of us and so aren't as rational as they imagine themselves to be. If only they'd exploit this new way of measuring utility directly they could take account of our irrationalities and non-monetary satisfactions, and get a much better fix on what individuals and policy-makers should be doing to raise our utility.

The economists' model assumes something even they know to be silly: that we regard work as a source of dis-utility. That is, we never enjoy work and put up with it solely for the utility we can buy with our wages. Unsurprisingly, the psychologists' measures of utility confirm that many of us derive considerable utility from the work we do which, among many other things, explains why sensible lottery winners don't give up their jobs and many older people continue working longer than they need to financially. As we saw in Chapter 5, and as Oxford economic historian Avner Offer explains in *The Challenge of Affluence*, work is a prime source of subjective wellbeing because of the many things it brings us: exercise of personal control, use of our skills, the need to respond to challenges, variety, a social context to exist in, supportive supervision, social contact and social status.

So the assumption that work is always unpleasant is a glaring weakness in the economists' model that they should correct because it continues to influence the conclusions of their analyses even though, in a different part of their brain, they know the proposition to be silly. Were they actually to build it into their models they'd be more cautious in proposing 'reforms' that would cause each of us to be a little better off in terms of having to pay lower prices, at the cost of probably protracted unemployment for a few of us.

We derive utility not only from work and social relations, but from self-determination and the use of our abilities and skills. And here's another thing economists find hard to take on board: we derive utility—happiness, as we'd say if we weren't talking econospeak—or dis-utility from processes, not just outcomes. So next time someone says, 'It wasn't what they did, it was the way they did it', you can believe them (even if they are also secretly offended by what was done).

One thing economists seek to bring consumers is wider choice. They see having a range of options to choose from as a benefit in itself. And they're right—up to a point. No one wants to live in a world where you can have any colour you want as long as it's black. But as Barry Schwartz, a professor of psychology at Swathmore College in Philadelphia, points out in his book *The Paradox of Choice*, because we're not the emotionless calculators economists assume us to be we lack the neural processing power to make any but reasonably simple choices. He tells of the experiment in which a stall was set up in a supermarket. On one occasion customers were offered samples of 24 different jams; on another occasion they were offered just six varieties. Ten times as many sales were made when only six varieties were offered, suggesting that, when people are offered excessive choice, they often avoid making any decision. In another experiment, people had difficulty choosing between the opposite attractions of flat A and flat B. But when the experimenters added flat C, which was similar to B but clearly inferior, a lot of people opted for B. They avoided the hard choice between A and B by substituting the easy choice between B and C, meaning that the addition of C acted as a decoy. Marketers and merchandisers have been exploiting this defect in our decision-making powers for centuries, even though economists are blinded to it by their assumption of rationality.

Our little problem with self-control

Another implication of our lack of rationality—and inability to correctly predict our utility—is the difficulty we have with self-control. The more affluent we in the rich countries become, the more our world abounds with temptations: to eat too much, get too little exercise, smoke, drink too much, watch too much television, gamble too much, shop too much, save too little, put too much on our credit cards, and work too much at the expense of our family and other relationships.

With all these things we know we shouldn't overindulge, but we often have terrible trouble making ourselves do the right thing. It's as though we have two selves: an unconscious self that's emotional and short-sighted, and a conscious self that's reasoning and far-sighted. We have trouble controlling ourselves in circumstances where the benefits are immediate and certain, whereas the costs are longer term and uncertain. As we saw in Chapter 2, everyone who's ever tried to diet, give up smoking, control their drinking, save or get on top of their credit card debt knows how hard it is to achieve the self-control our conscious, future-selves want us to achieve.

One reason for taking the problem of self-control so seriously is the likelihood that the very success of the market system in making us more affluent is serving to heighten our self-control problem. Our brains work the way they do as a result of our evolution and the historical need to cope with the problem of scarcity. Economics is all about coping with scarcity. But human ingenuity—including the development of the market system—has increasingly overcome scarcity. These days, most of us in the developed economies have a greater problem coping with abundance than scarcity. For instance, we've evolved to eat everything that comes our way. However, where food was once scarce it is now abundant and, hence, cheap, so we've lost the externally imposed constraint that, until relatively recently, stopped our instinct to overeat from making us overweight. Similarly, the huge growth in our real incomes over the past century has made it easier for us to afford to overindulge in many of the other vices I listed. Credit is another thing that's become readily available and relatively cheap, with deregulated banks now keen to lend and credit cards ubiquitous.

So I'm beginning to think that overindulgence and difficulties in self-control are the big problem of our age. Even the worries we have about our despoiling of the environment and our excess emissions of greenhouse gases can be seen as problems of abundance. Too much unguided economic activity—which has also led to too much population growth—is upsetting the Earth's natural balance. Chapter 8 is devoted to the conflict between economic growth and the environment, which is another significant instance of the narrow focus of economics causing it to fail to take account of the subsequent advances of science—in this case, ecology, the study of the relationships between organisms and their environments.

People know they have trouble controlling themselves, trouble allowing their future-selves to dominate their present-selves and so avoid myopic choices. The way to do this is by developing 'commitment strategies' and 'commitment devices'. Economists need to understand the need for and accept the legitimacy of commitment devices, which come at three levels. First, the restrictions individuals choose to impose on their own behaviour. Second, the restrictions the members of groups choose to impose on themselves by adherence to group norms of acceptable behaviour. Third, the restrictions governments impose on us to remove temptation from our paths.

Economists have trouble coming to terms with each of the three levels. With self-imposed commitment devices, conventionally trained economists are tempted to regard them as irrational behaviour. I may try to limit my consumption of ice cream by keeping only one small serve in the fridge. Should I want to eat more than my allocated daily limit, I have to go the shop and get it. Technically, this behaviour is inefficient and irrational: it's cheaper and easier to buy ice cream in bigger quantities.

With group-imposed behavioural norms or codes of behaviour, conventional economists often aren't conscious of their existence or don't appreciate their value until some economic upheaval destroys them. Increased competitive pressures in business, for instance, can cause a breakdown in professional standards of behaviour towards clients.

With government-imposed restrictions, the conventional economists' assumption that individuals behave rationally— that is, always in their own best interests—leads them to disapprove of many government interventions. How could governments know better than individuals what was in those individuals' best interests? Why not leave people free to choose for themselves? Short answer: because individuals know they have trouble controlling themselves and would appreciate government taking temptation out of their way. In practice, we see any amount of often quite punitive government intervention aimed at protecting both the individual and the community from the consequences of speeding on the road, excessive drinking, smoking, air and water pollution, drug use, gambling, usury, and much else. It's notable that most of these impositions on our freedom were introduced without great opposition and today are quite uncontroversial. Why do we accept these restrictions so readily? Because we—and the politicians who impose them—know they help us control our more myopic selves.

As well as such coercive interventions there are less intrusive ways governments and others can change behaviour merely by changing the way choices are 'framed'. For instance, in encouraging employees to join voluntary saving schemes, automatically enrolling them but permitting them to opt out will be far more successful than inviting them to opt in. Economists can master these behavioural tricks.

But let's return to individuals imposing their own commitment devices. In his book *Mindless Eating*, the Cornell psychologist Brian Wansink writes that the 19th century has been called the Century of Hygiene and the 20th century the Century of Medicine. This century, he predicts, will be the Century of Behavioural Change. Changing your personal behaviour isn't easy, but it is possible. It involves adopting better habits, which eventually become part of our unconscious selves and so become lasting. Jonathan Haidt says that trying to control yourself is like riding an elephant. The elephant has a mind of its own and can't just be ordered to obey. It can, however, be carefully trained and cajoled into more desirable ways.

Whatever you think is a fair thing

Because it focuses on 'the problem of scarcity'—the contention that, though the resources at society's disposal are strictly finite, our wants are infinite—conventional economics is preoccupied with the need for greater 'efficiency' in the way scarce resources are allocated to different uses. Its model ignores the question of fairness (also called 'equity') of the distribution of resources, or of the income that gives command over resources, between different individuals or families within the society.

A decent economics course will include some consideration of the principles of fairness, such as those enunciated by the Harvard moral philosopher John Rawls, but in practice consideration of fairness is often a victim of model blindness—it's not in the model so it tends to be downplayed, if not completely overlooked in public policy prescriptions. When economists are taxed on this question they often reply that they're silent on the equity implications of their recommendations because it's an area outside their field of competence. They leave it for the politicians to decide. But in advocating their one-dimensional solutions to problems, they often fail to issue a consumer warning about the narrowness and incompleteness of their perspective.

Research by psychologists leaves little doubt that people are very much concerned with questions of fairness. Economists are adept at keeping efficiency and equity considerations in separate boxes, but people aren't—and don't see why they should. Consider a laboratory experiment called the ultimatum game. You're offered $100. All you have to do is agree with someone else how you'll share it between you. But here's the trick: you get only one chance to propose how it be split and, if the other person doesn't accept your proposal, both of you end up with nothing. What's more, you're in separate rooms, so you can't discuss an acceptable deal.

So, how would *you* split it? Economic theory says that's a no-brainer. Because it assumes Homo economicus is selfish and rational, it predicts that you'll want to keep almost all the $100 for yourself and leave very little for the other guy. And it confidently predicts the other guy will say yes. He or she won't like it, but they won't consider saying no. Why not? Because the other guy is also selfish and rational. And even if you offer as little as $1, they'll say yes because $1 is better than nothing.

Wrong. About two thirds of the time the other person is offered between 40 and 50 per cent of the money. Only four people in 100 offer less than 20 per cent. And more than half of such offers are rejected. So people aren't nearly as selfish, nor as 'rational' as economists assume. They treat the other person more generously than assumed and they're perfectly prepared to walk away from money rather than accept a deal they regard as unfair.

Ernst Fehr, a professor of economics at the University of Zurich, summarised what we've learnt about our attitudes to fairness in an article he wrote with some colleagues in the January 2002 issue of the *Scientific American*. For a start, note that when the proposer in the ultimatum game is picked not by the flip of a coin but by having done better in a quiz, they're more inclined to give themselves a bigger share. And the responder is more inclined to accept it. In this case, because the proposer is perceived to have been picked on merit, it's not seen as unfair for them to get a larger slice.

Now let's look at another experiment, called the public goods game. Four separated players are given $20 each and asked to decide how much to invest in a common pool. The experimenter doubles the money in the pool and shares it equally between the players. You can see this is a co-operation game. The more the group co-operates, the better off it is. Were every player to put into the pool the whole of their $20, everyone would be twice as well off. But what's true for the group as a whole isn't true for the individual. If you put in while I shirk, I still get my quarter of the gain from your contribution.

So the individual faces a great temptation to be a 'free-rider' on the group. But the more people in the group yield to that temptation, the worse it is for everyone. Were every individual to be completely 'rational' and contribute nothing to the pool, no one would gain anything from the magic of public goods. Thankfully, people aren't so selfish. Repeated experiments with this game show that most people invest at least half their money.

When you keep repeating the game with the same players, they do eventually start cutting back their contributions. But this seems to be not so much because they're learning the benefits of free-riding as because they're reacting negatively to the perceived 'cheating' of the other players. Indeed, when you put these experienced players into new groups, they start out again by contributing a lot.

Then there's a variation on the game where a player can, for a fee, punish another player. I could reduce your money by $1, for instance, but it would cost me 30 cents. (The experimenter would remove $1.30 from the game.) According to the economists' model, this would be highly irrational behaviour. But players are actually very keen to pay the price necessary to punish people who contribute less than the rest of the group. It seems that players are motivated more by the satisfaction they get from punishing free-riders than by the monetary benefit they get by minimising free-riding.

In consequence, in repeated games with penalties contributions to the pool stay high. Contributions even rise as the game progresses. One moral of this story is that, being social animals, we care deeply about the behaviour of people around us: how they're faring compared with how we're faring.

Other research confirms that people have strong opinions not just about how things end up, but also about 'procedural fairness'—how the outcome was arrived at. Much to the bemusement of economists, most people object to shopkeepers raising the price of an item that's suddenly in high demand, such as snow shovels the morning after a large snowstorm. Economists regard such behaviour not only as the way the world has always worked, but also as the way it should work.

About three quarters of people in a survey regarded such behaviour—'rationing by price'—as unfair, whereas only a quarter of respondents regarded rationing on a first-come, first-served basis as unfair. In another study, employees' reactions to pay cuts are less adverse if they occur through fair processes, such as management thoroughly and sensitively explaining the basis for the cut.

Social capital? Oh, *that* social capital

Because the neoclassical model focuses so heavily on prices and the factors that cause them to change, another important area that tends to go unnoticed and unappreciated by economists is what they call 'institutions'—when they remember.

The term 'institutions' covers laws and the organisations appointed to govern commercial behaviour, as well as social norms. Even though they've been left out of the conventional model—making them prone to being subject to model blindness—institutions are critical to the efficient functioning of markets. Institutions such as the well-enforced law of contract, bankruptcy law, accounting standards and trustworthy auditors are taken for granted in developed economies but are vitally, if boringly, important. Economists' failure to understand this simple truth led to them having a hand in some terrible disasters in recent times, such as the Asian financial crisis of 1997–98 (where developing countries with utterly inadequate commercial infrastructure were urged to open their financial markets to hugely destabilising 'hot money' flows of foreign capital), and the badly botched transition to capitalism of Russia and other formerly planned economies.

More interestingly, a social norm is a form of behaviour caused by a widely shared belief in the appropriate way to behave. It often triggers informal social sanctions to enforce the prescribed behaviour. One social norm is that people should behave fairly towards others, and the previously described experiment in which players were willing to pay a fee to punish free-riders is an example of social sanctions intended to enforce socially appropriate behaviour.

Studies of wellbeing—or, if you like, utility—find that people who are unemployed are particularly unhappy, more so than can be explained by the loss of income involved. This suggests that the unemployed feel internal pressure to comply with the norm to work and not be dependent on others. Just how bad people feel about being jobless—and how hard they try to find a job and are willing to accept one that's far from ideal—is influenced by how strongly the community in which they live feels that living off public funds is wrong. We also know that unemployed people who live in areas of high unemployment don't feel as bad as those living in areas of low unemployment.

A community's 'social capital' concerns the social norms and networks that facilitate co-operation within or between groups. One element of social capital is trust. The more trust there is in marriages and social relations, the happier people are likely to be. I realised the *economic* value of trust years ago when I stepped off a plane in New York, picked up my bag from the carousel and was heading off to find a taxi when a burly security guard stopped me and asked to see the luggage tickets that proved the bag I'd taken was mine. The more trustworthy a community is, the more we can keep the wheels of commerce turning without the expense of doing more checking, increasing security, taking out insurance, trying to write watertight contracts, consulting lawyers and going to court.

For businesses (and individuals, for that matter) the antidote to mistrust is reputation. To have a reputation for delivering value for money and being willing to correct mistakes promptly and courteously is money in the bank. That's why businesses place so much emphasis on brand names and—if they have any sense—work hard to protect their brands' reputations.

Trust and loyalty are closely related. Much customer trust and loyalty to our banks had built up before they were deregulated in the 1980s, but the pressure of increased competition tempted the banks to exploit their customers' loyalty, particularly by neglecting to inform their existing customers of the better deals they were offering to attract new customers.

Employees frequently derive satisfaction from feelings of loyalty towards their employers, but in recent years this has not been reciprocated by public companies anxious to impress the sharemarket by announcing big rounds of redundancies. Customer and employee loyalty is a valuable asset to businesses, but when they act in ways that take advantage of that loyalty they make short-term gains at the expense of long-term costs. The point is that the economists' model does nothing to warn businesses of the choices they face, nor to alert governments to these hidden potential costs of 'reform'.

The market versus the community

In practice, conventional economics is about studying and promoting the role of the market. But according to Stephen Marglin, a professor of economics at Harvard, in his book *The Dismal Science*, economics has been shaped by an agenda focused on showing that markets are good for people rather than on discovering how markets actually work. It's important to understand the distinction between 'the market' and 'markets'. Humans have been using markets to exchange goods and services for millennia, long before economists popped up, and will probably go on using markets for as long as this planet lasts. By contrast, 'the market' is all the markets in a country, which economists see as a (supposedly) self-regulating *system* for allocating resources and distributing income and wealth.

It's not the existence of markets but the adulation of The Market that's questionable. Paradoxically, while many academic economists are inward-looking and little interested in using their discipline to solve real-world problems, other economists—some of them academics, but particularly business and bureaucratic economists—and their politically inspired fellow travellers are quite imperialistic, continuously advocating that more and more aspects of our daily lives be handed over to the market. Such an ideology sits well with many business people, who are always looking for new ways to make a quid. Apart from the privatising of many government-owned businesses in recent decades, we've

witnessed the commercialisation—some call it the commodi-
fication—of sport, childcare, aged care, universities, training for
foreign students, public broadcasting (ads on SBS, though not
yet the ABC), and the outsourcing of the government's job-
placement service to businesses and charities alike. At present the
line has been drawn at legalising the markets for sexual services
and drugs, and commercialising the provision of blood, body
parts and surrogate motherhood.

Economists are committed to the market because they're
convinced it's the best way to achieve greater efficiency in the
allocation of resources, which leads to faster growth in
the economy and a higher material standard of living. And the
truth is that, within their own narrow objectives, they're right.
Since the days of the Industrial Revolution, the market system—
guided broadly by the precepts of conventional economics—has
raised living standards many times over. Much of that improvement is owed to scientific discovery and technological advance,
but these developments have been fostered by the capitalist
system.

Stephen Marglin acknowledges that much good has come
with economic growth: 'longer lives, less physical discomfort and
even less pain, better nutrition and less hard physical toil to
mention only a few of the positives'. The list of remarkable electronic devices that have come our way even just in recent
decades—and at ever-moderating prices—is long: colour, high-
definition and digital television; microwave ovens; digital
photography and movie cameras and electronic games; personal
computers, the internet and email; mobile phones with built-in
messaging, cameras and internet access.

Have these things raised our *objective* wellbeing? Undoubtedly.
Have they raised our *subjective* wellbeing? Probably not, thanks to

rapid adaptation—but both sides of the story need to be acknowledged. And despite all the sneering, the truth is that the benefits *have* trickled down to people at the bottom of the pile. Material living standards in the developed world have been rising for 200 years. Is it seriously contended that, in all that time, incomes have risen at the top but not the bottom? They've risen at all levels, with the gap between rich and poor actually narrowing until the 1970s, since which it has widened again in many rich countries.

This widespread sharing of our ever-growing affluence explains why the rich countries long ago switched to measuring poverty in relative rather than absolute terms. A rise in the relative poverty rate—and a widening in the dispersion of incomes between the top and the bottom, for that matter—signifies only that real incomes haven't risen as fast at the bottom as they have at the top. The unshakable belief that 'the poor have got poorer' is simply factually inaccurate.

It's true that market economies go through cycles and boom and bust. Always have and probably always will. But the fact that when boom turns to bust and share prices and (in some countries) house prices crash while unemployment rises doesn't mean it was all for nought. When you average out the ups and downs of the business cycle, the long-term trend of rising material living standards remains.

So what's the problem? Well, most economists, business people and politicians can't see one. But that's because the neoclassic model—and the conventional means of measuring progress—doesn't register any. In every other part of economics no choice comes without an opportunity cost, there are always costs to be weighed against benefits and the goal is to optimise rather than maximise variables. But none of that applies—apparently—when it comes to economic growth. Here there are no costs and the more growth the better, forever and ever.

The problem is that economists' conventional means of measuring progress simply don't register the costs. That's mainly because most of the costs are non-monetary, and non-monetary factors aren't in the model. It also seems likely that, as several centuries of technological advance have allowed market economies to overcome the problem of scarcity—changing our greatest challenges to those that accompany affluence, as Avner Offer has argued—economics has been overtaken by the very success of the market system it champions. In other words, as the material benefits have grown, so have the non-material costs. Such a relationship—roughly akin to diminishing marginal returns—is actually quite familiar in economic analysis.

So what is the cost? Stephen Marglin argues it's the loss of community. The distinctive feature of community, he says, is that it provides a kind of social glue, binding people together in relationships that give form and flavour to life. (And, of course, the very stuff that the happiness research tells us adds so much to our subjective wellbeing.) By the same token, Stephen adds, community depends on constraints and obligations that transcend the calculation of individual utility.

Markets are the cutting edge of the loss of human connection. Economists see this as a virtue because impersonal markets accomplish more efficiently what the connections of social solidarity, reciprocity and other redistributive institutions do in less commercialised societies. Consider Stephen's example of fire insurance versus barn-raising. 'I pay a premium of, say, $200 per year, and if my barn burns down the insurance company pays me $60,000 to rebuild it. A simple market transaction has replaced the cumbersome process of gathering my neighbours for a barn-raising. In terms of building barns with a minimal expenditure of resources, insurance may indeed be more efficient than gathering the community each time somebody's barn burns down. But in terms of maintaining the community, insurance is woefully lacking,' Stephen says.

The argument is that increasing our reliance on impersonal markets may well be more efficient, so that it does indeed raise our material standard of living, but that this comes at the less-visible cost of breaking down the social connections that contribute so much to our personal happiness.

Stephen argues that every time a good or service is turned into something that's bought and sold, the result is to substitute impersonal market relationships for personal relationships of reciprocity and the like. Against this, some economists have offered the ingenious argument that using the market to accomplish the basic tasks of life frees up energy for other ways of connecting. What does the economist economise? they ask. That scarce resource, love—which economists know just as well as anybody else is the most precious thing in the world. Nice try. Trouble is, love is like muscles—to retain them they have to be exercised regularly. And the more you exercise them the better they work.

One issue that's long dismayed me is the way weekends and public holidays are being taken over by the market. You and I quite like the convenience of being able to shop, eat out or be commercially entertained at the weekend. And, at least until recently, employers had much success at making this more economical by persuading governments, industrial courts and even workers that to require penalty wage rates as compensation for employees being required to work at 'unsociable hours' was now quite antediluvian. The very term 'unsociable' gives the game away. For those people required to work on weekends or public holidays, the result is less leisure time spent with spouses, families and friends, and more leisure time spent alone. That's a step forward? On balance, I doubt it.

A more recent fear of mine is that the economic reform-caused increase in competitive pressure in so many markets, and the related less-constrained pursuit of monetary rewards, is leading to a decline in ethical behaviour and the peer-group social norms and sanctions that formerly reinforced it. It seems that, as competitive pressure has intensified, the old standards of behaviour have been tipped overboard as niceties that can no longer be afforded. And as the most aggressive competitors have greatly increased their incomes, others have been induced to play by the new rules. There was a time when being 'professional' meant putting your clients' interests ahead of your own. Today the word usually just means being good at your job. Since it's hard to impose ethical behaviour by legislation, this decline into more ruthless behaviour is an unintended, unmeasured and even unacknowledged social cost to be set against the benefits of greater efficiency.

The mismeasurement of wellbeing

Economists get annoyed whenever non-economists lecture them about the weaknesses of GDP—gross domestic product—the measure that's come to be treated as the definitive indicator of national wellbeing. Why the annoyance? Because no one understands the conceptual limitations of GDP better than an economist. Whatever non-economists know on that topic must have come originally from an economist. And every economist knows that GDP isn't a measure of wellbeing, nor was it ever intended to be.

But that doesn't get economists off the hook. The truth is that, however much they know about the limitations of GDP, they have no great mission to point these out to people. Nor has the profession demonstrated much desire to develop improved measures. Rather, economists have done more than most to encourage the uninitiated to focus on movements in GDP—indeed, the quarterly rate of change in GDP—as the single most important indicator of (undefined) progress.

GDP is the bottom line of what economists grandly refer to as 'the national accounts'. What it actually measures is the value of the nation's total production of goods and services during a period, which is equivalent to the nation's income for that period. But it's not even a perfect measure of this because, where the private sector's concerned, it measures the production only of those goods and services that change hands in the marketplace and so have a price put on them. This means it doesn't include the value of services provided by volunteers and, far more significantly, the huge quantity of goods and services produced and consumed inside the home. When a man marries his housekeeper this is recorded as a decline in GDP because, whereas the wage he paid the housekeeper was counted as adding to national income, the work a wife does within the home is not counted towards GDP.

But even if it were a perfect measure of production and income it would still be a misleading measure of anything approximating wellbeing. For one thing, it includes spending on 'regrettable necessities'—sometimes known as 'defensive expenditure'—occasioned by the actual or anticipated *destruction* of utility: the cost of preventing or cleaning up after road accidents, and the costs of police protection, road maintenance, sanitation and defence. Why include all those unfortunate necessities?

Because, however regrettable they may be, they nonetheless involve the generation of income for the people who work in those industries.

Next, GDP, having been formulated in the 1940s, makes no serious attempt to take account of the cost of the damage that our economic activity does to the natural environment. Although it includes money governments and others spend trying to *reduce* pollution (again, because this activity generates income for people), it doesn't allow for the cost of the long-term damage done by the pollution itself (including the effects of emissions of greenhouse gases into the atmosphere) nor for the cost of the using up of non-renewable resources or the overexploitation of renewable resources such as fish.

But even all that doesn't cover the full reasons GDP doesn't measure up as a measure of wellbeing. It doesn't take account of adverse—or even favourable—changes in the way the nation's income is *distributed* between individuals or families, even though this clearly has big effects on individuals' happiness. Worse, it takes no account of the non-monetary, non-material consequences of human activity. Is the growth in incomes coming at the expense of reduced leisure? We may be buying a little more because shops are open seven days a week, but what's that doing to the family lives of people who have to work at weekends? What's happening to social capital and community?

In recent years a number of the leading psychologists in happiness research—including Ed Diener and Martin Seligman—have been campaigning for governments to produce 'national wellbeing accounts'. Understandably, they want to lift the sights of the makers of public policy above economic growth to the many non-monetary factors that have such a bearing on the subjective wellbeing of a nation's citizens. Let's stop deluding ourselves that if GDP's on the up and up, all's right with the world.

Since GDP is so misleading, wouldn't it be nice if we could replace it with an accurate measure of national wellbeing? It would be, but I doubt it's possible. It's very human to seek a single, all-encompassing measure of progress, and this does much to explain the excessive authority the public invests in GDP. But for widely disparate factors to be added together into a single indicator, they each have to be capable of being converted to a common denominator. In practice, much violence can be done to indicators in this conversion process and you're almost invariably left with factors that end up being excluded— and thus ignored—because they simply can't be incorporated. This, of course, is the underlying problem with GDP.

But I think the psychologists understand this. They want national accounts of wellbeing to parallel the national economic accounts, not replace them. (As a measure of short-term movements in national income, GDP has its place as an indicator to assist in the day-to-day management of the economy.) But they believe—correctly—that societies tend to take notice of things that are measured and take steps towards improving numbers that are too low. So they suggest areas of life that could usefully be measured more regularly and more prominently, without suggesting that they all need to be added together in some way.

Such as? It would be good to track whether kids are happier or less happy than they were in the past, identifying which classes of kids are having problems. Are segments of the child population becoming more stressed or depressed while other segments are flourishing? In their book *Happiness*, Ed Diener and his son say we could also track which workers are engaged and which hate their work, and why.

Another question is whether there are pockets of misery—say, among certain ethnic communities, or among groups such as carers for the elderly or handicapped—that need special attention from governments. And are there certain activities—commuting by car would be a prime suspect—that are causing increased stress and lower life satisfaction in modern societies? As these examples imply, the best way for governments to maximise national wellbeing may be to focus on measures to reduce significant instances of ill-being.

In the aftermath of the global financial crisis, and at the instigation of President Nicolas Sarkozy of France, an international group of eminent economists, led by the Nobel laureates Joseph Stiglitz and Amartya Sen—with support from such names as Kenneth Arrow, James Heckman and Daniel Kahneman—has inquired into the measurement of 'economic performance and social progress'. Their report concluded that 'the time is ripe for our measurement system to shift emphasis from measuring economic production to measuring people's wellbeing'.

After proposing improvements in the national accounts to better measure *material* wellbeing, the report proposes the better and more regular measurement of other dimensions of wellbeing including health, education, personal activities including work, political voice and governance, social connections and relationships, the environment (present and future), and insecurity of both an economic and a physical nature. But as well as these measures of *objective* wellbeing, the report finds it's also possible to collect meaningful and reliable data on *subjective* wellbeing. So government statisticians should include in their own surveys questions about people's life evaluations, positive and negative emotions and priorities.

The report says measuring and assessing sustainability—the ability for at least the present level of wellbeing to be maintained for future generations—is a central concern, which should be considered separately from measures of present wellbeing. 'The environmental aspects of sustainability deserve a separate follow-up based on a well-chosen set of physical indicators. In particular there is a need for a clear indicator of our proximity to dangerous levels of environmental damage (such as associated with climate change or the depletion of fishing stocks),' the report concludes.

To have such a prestigious group of economists come to such forthright and enlightened conclusions is encouraging. Perhaps matters are at last starting to move in the right direction. I fear, however, it may be a long time before their views have much tangible impact in the corridors of statistical power. And even were we to reach a point where a much more balanced range of indicators was brought together and published in many countries, there would still be the question of whether this could share much of the attention with that great god, GDP.

Get your retaliation in first

I have to tell you that most economists will be quite unimpressed and unconvinced by this critique of their discipline. They've heard it all before and, like all of us, their first reaction to criticism is to become defensive. One reaction will be that, whatever the merits of my criticism of their model, if it can't be encapsulated in mathematics then whether it's right or wrong is of little relevance to their professional endeavours.

Another defensive reaction is that, whatever the criticism, the profession has already got it covered. You say that conventional economics ignores issues of fairness? Nonsense, I've included a lecture about Rawlsian principles in my course for years. You say that protracted economic growth in the rich countries seems to have done little to increase subjective wellbeing? That paradox was first highlighted by an economist, Dick Easterlin. You say psychology has poked holes in the neoclassical assumption of rational decision-making? Economics has a whole new strand of inquiry—behavioural economics—exploring the implications of psychological research into decision-making.

Sorry, not convinced. These are just excuses. It's true that none of the criticisms I've aired is new and that many of them have been articulated by economists. So I'll be accused of setting up a straw man, a caricature of economics that's oversimplified and woefully out of date. But the economists whose work is appealed to by the defenders are operating on the lonely fringes of professional orthodoxy. Stephen Marglin says the enterprise of economics is better characterised by the content of elementary textbooks than by what goes on at the frontiers of economic theory. Just so, and the economic model I've described is the one being taught to students in classrooms and lecture theatres across the world. It's also the one that most influences the thinking of economic policy-makers.

As we've seen, mainstream economists believe in 'revealed preference': ignore what people *say* they'd like to do and judge their preferences solely by what they actually do with their money. I think revealed preference is one of economics' great bum steers. But I do think it's a decision rule we can turn back on the economists themselves: ignore what they say they know all about and judge them by the decisions they make and the policies they urge on politicians and the public. If you judge their beliefs by their works, I'm confident you'll find they believe what I've said they believe.

The non-material bottom line

Economics' preoccupation with efficiency and economic growth has made it too focused on the material and oblivious to the non-material dimensions of life. As Stephen Marglin says, 'that which affects the values, attitudes, behaviours and ways of inter-acting with other people lies outside the economist's ken'. Economists have lost sight of the fact that material consumption and GDP are merely means to an end, not an end in itself. What we should be aiming for is improved human wellbeing, broadly defined, which must also be sustainable in the light of the immense ecological difficulties we face.

The goals of economics need to be reoriented to make them broader and sustainable. It needs to be based on better models of human nature and of how the economy fits within the environment. Since that couldn't be achieved in short order, economists should stop pontificating and predicting on the basis of such a flawed model and devote their energy to empirical study of the way the world actually does work. But such reform is unlikely. In which case, the public must learn to give less weight to the opinions of economists and set their advice against that of social scientists and ecologists with a firmer grip on the realities of our complex, multidimensional world.

8

THE ECONOMY AND THE ENVIRONMENT

What have future generations ever done for me?
— An economist we must hope was joking

How do you picture the economy? If you had to depict it with a drawing or a diagram, what would it look like? I suspect that, after giving it some thought, most people would depict the economy as a box in which businesses on one side produced goods and services that they sold to households on the other. The households would pay for the goods and services they consumed mainly by selling their labour to the businesses doing the producing. Certainly, that's the way economists have schooled us to think of the economy: an endless round of production and consumption.

Now let's say you're asked to add the environment to the diagram—how would you do it? I think most people would just draw another box for it, maybe with arrows going between the two boxes. Again, that's the way most economists think about it and have encouraged us to think about it. But in his book *Beyond Growth* Herman Daly, a professor of economics at the University of Maryland, says this is quite a mistaken and misleading way to think of the relationship between the economy and the environment.

In his depiction, the environment is a big circle while the economy is a box *inside* the circle. His point—simple, but profound—is that the economy exists *within* the natural environment. The environment could exist without the economy, but the economy couldn't exist without a natural environment to exist in. The global economy is thus just a subsystem of what Herman calls the global ecosystem.

Why is it so important to see the economy as existing within the ecosystem? Because the ecosystem provides humans' life-support. It does three things for the economy that the economy couldn't do for itself. First, it provides natural resources, such as food, fibre, fuel, biological diversity and drugs. Second, it performs essential 'ecological services' for the economy, such as photosynthesis, regulation of atmospheric gas, water and climate, formation of soil and control of pests. Third, the ecosystem absorbs our wastes—including sewage and garbage but, in fact, all fluids, solids, gases and heat. The first law of thermodynamics says that energy can be changed from one form to another, but it can't be created or destroyed. So what the economic system does from a physicist's perspective is it takes natural resources (matter) and turns them into waste.

But another reason it's so important to see the economy as existing within the ecosystem is that the global economy is an open, growing system, whereas the global ecosystem—the Earth—is fixed in size. It doesn't grow. It receives no new flows of materials, though it does receive a continuous (fixed) flow of energy from the sun. So if the global economy can grow—which it is doing, exponentially (that is, by a constant percentage each year, rather than by a constant absolute amount)—whereas the ecosystem in which it exists can't, it's clear there must be limits to the extent to which the economy can grow. The question is whether the global economy's growth is sustainable—able to be continued in the same form for many years without doing damage to the ecosystem.

The effects of economic activity

All human activity—most of which can be classed as economic activity, in the sense that it involves either the production or the consumption of goods and services—has adverse effects on the environment. As the famous economist Jeffrey Sachs, of Columbia University, explains in his book *Common Wealth: Economics for a Crowded Planet*, our species' natural history is not merely one of human migration and population growth. Our deepest pattern has been the appropriation of the Earth's natural systems for human use, often at great and unwitting cost to other species and to the long-term wellbeing of human society.

'Nature provides us with the stuff of life—food, water, fuels, fibres—and human society has worked relentlessly to harness nature's services to support a rising human population and rising levels of consumption per person, but typically unaware of the long-term consequences,' he writes.

Some scientists contend that, even before humans abandoned hunting and gathering to take up farming about 10,000 years ago, they had hunted the mega-fauna to the point of extinction. Jeff says the shift to agriculture represented a qualitative change to the natural order, one whose consequences are still being played out. In an agricultural system, the land is cleared of natural communities of plants and animals so that the solar energy can be appropriated by humans in a more direct manner.

Photosynthesis produces the foodstuffs directly consumed by humans, or foodstuffs consumed by domesticated animals that are directly consumed by humans. The balance between humans and the rest of the biosphere was decisively altered. Human populations soared.

But nothing in human history prepared humanity or the Earth for what happened after about 1800, the start of the Industrial Revolution. At that point we entered the age of the Anthropocene—when human activity became the dominant driver of the natural environment. Since then, Jeff says, humanity has lived off the treasure trove of hoarded solar power that is packaged in fossil fuels.

The human impact on the environment (I) can be broken into three parts: the total population (P), average income per person (A, for affluence) and the environmental impact per dollar of income (T, for the level of technology). This is sometimes called the I-PAT equation. Since the start of the Industrial Revolution we've seen a dramatic rise in population. At the time of the introduction of agriculture, 8000 BC, the global human population was perhaps 10 million. By AD 1 it was about 230 million; by 1800 it had reached 1 billion. The next billion took about 120 years, taking us to 1922. The one after that took 37 years, taking us to 1959, and after that the billions kept coming every 15 years or less. By 2000 we'd hit 6 billion, and today we're at 6.6 billion.

The technological advances of the industrial age—many of them powered by fossil fuels—raised the productivity of workers to previously unimaginable levels. So the takeoff in population was matched by a simultaneous takeoff in average economic production per person, represented by income per person.

According to the best estimates available, world income per person changed little between 1500 and the start of the Industrial Revolution, but by the second half of the 1800s reached $1000 a year (all measured in US dollars of 1990 purchasing power). By about 1950 world average income reached $2000, and by 2001, $6000. (In the developed countries, average incomes were very much higher than that, of course.)

Jeff says that a tenfold increase in human population since 1750 and a similar increase in production per person mean that economic activity is perhaps one hundred times what it was at the start of the industrial era. As for the present state of technology, you'd have to say it's a lot more oriented towards fully exploiting the natural environment than protecting it from harm.

Jeff lists 'six Earth-changing trends, unprecedented in human history'. First, the process of sustained economic growth has now reached most of the world, so humanity on average is rapidly getting richer in terms of income per person. Believe it or not, with the spread of capitalist economics to many countries in Asia, South America and the former communist countries of Eastern Europe, the gap in average income per person between the rich world and much of the developing world is narrowing fast. Although the growth in the world's population means the *number* of people living in absolute poverty is pretty much higher than ever before, the *proportion* of the world's population living in absolute poverty has fallen from perhaps 85 per cent before the Industrial Revolution to 50 per cent by 1950, 25 per cent in 1992 and to 15 per cent before the onset of the global financial crisis.

Second, the world's population will continue to rise, thereby amplifying the overall growth of the global economy. From 6.6 billion today, the United Nations medium projection says it will reach 9.3 billion by 2050 (although slowly falling fertility rates suggest it will stabilise later in the century). Add to that continuing growth in productivity per person and—assuming away environmental catastrophe—the scale of the world's economic production could be several times what it is today.

Third, the rise in income will be greatest in Asia, home to more than half the world's population. As a result, the world will not only be much richer by 2050, its economic centre of gravity will have moved to Asia. China and India alone account for almost 40 per cent of the world's population. If their economies continue growing by 7 per cent a year—which seems plausible—they will double in size every decade.

Fourth, the way people live is changing fundamentally around the world, from rural roots that stretch back to the beginning of humanity to a global urban civilisation. We crossed the halfway point between rural and urban in 2008. Jeff says that, when agricultural productivity is high—so that a farm family can feed many urban residents—a significant share of the population is able to live in urban areas and engage in producing manufactures or services.

Fifth, the gap between the richest and poorest people in the world is widening to proportions unimaginable for most people. This is true even though, as we have seen, the poor are getting richer on average. The bottom one billion people on the planet are stuck in a poverty trap, which has prevented them from experiencing sustained economic growth. The centre of this crisis is sub-Saharan Africa. Jeff says this is also the site of the fastest population growth, so that the population bulge is occurring in the part of the world least able to generate jobs.

Sixth, the overall impact of human activity on the physical environment is producing multiple ecological crises as never before in history. The environmental crises we face can't be compared with the past because never before in history has the magnitude of human economic activity been large enough to change fundamental natural processes on a global scale.

Evidence of environmental damage

There is now a mass of evidence of the damage economic activity is doing to the ecosystem. Foremost in our mind is the way, after 200 years, the burning of fossil fuels and clearing of forests have led to emissions of carbon dioxide and other gases which have built up in the atmosphere and are now causing global warming and changing the climate in other ways.

But the evidence of severe environmental damage extends far wider than this. As Herman Daly reminds us, even something as seemingly insignificant as a tree delivers a host of vital ecosystem services: it sequesters (removes and stores) carbon dioxide, provides wildlife habitat, controls soil erosion and provides local cooling. Clear a lot of forests, cut down a lot of trees, and many bad things happen. Evidence summarised by Dr Alan Jones, of the Australian Museum, finds that every year around the world about 26 billion tonnes of topsoil are lost, 6 million hectares of primary forest are cleared and deserts expand by 6 million hectares.

Two thirds of the world's agricultural land suffers soil degradation, 40 per cent of it seriously. Forty to 50 per cent of the land surface has been irreversibly transformed and productive land per person has fallen from more than five hectares in 1900 to less than 1.5 hectares in 1995. Much of the world's agriculture is dependent on oil and irrigation by ground water, both of which are being depleted rapidly.

Turning to water, the past century has seen half the world's wetlands lost, nearly 40,000 large dams built affecting 60 per cent of the largest rivers, 54 per cent of accessible freshwater runoff appropriated by humans, and the quality and quantity of available surface water and ground water fall.

About half of all monitored fish stocks is now fully exploited and another quarter is overexploited, depleted or slowly recovering. Only the remaining quarter is underexploited or moderately exploited, leading to the conclusion that the global maximum potential for marine-capture fisheries has been reached and passed, with restrictive management measures now needed. There is thus little hope that fisheries can be expanded to help feed the growing population.

Take virtually any habitat on the planet, Jeff Sachs says, and we find that the non-human species in it are under unprecedented stress for multiple reasons. Their habitats are being overtaken by cropland, pollution, overhunting and overharvesting, invasive species and new pests and pathogens. When disastrous thresholds are reached, such as the mass die-off of amphibian species in many parts of the world, there are so many specific culprits that a single cause can't be established. The massive threats to species survival are not due to land clearing or water stress or pollution or invasive species alone, but to all of them combined, with interacting and amplifying effects.

Will coral reefs survive the 21st century? Jeff Sachs asks. Global warming will raise ocean temperatures and lead to widespread coral bleaching, and reefs will be threatened by overfishing, by pollution, by increased tropical storm intensity, by direct destruction by tourists, and by ocean acidification due to the rising concentration of carbon dioxide in the air and ocean surface water.

Turning to biodiversity, Alan Jones says humans are responsible for the sixth major extinction event in the entire history of the Earth. The rate of species loss exceeds 100 times the natural rate. As well, genetic diversity has declined because many species have suffered large population declines. This has caused a third of amphibians, an eighth of birds and one in four mammals to be at risk of extinction. Fresh waters and forests are particularly vulnerable, with one fifth of all freshwater species and one tenth of tree species being extinct or endangered.

Many of these damaging trends can be found in Australia. In 200 years, Europeans have changed natural habitats greatly. Indeed, when it comes to the clearing of vegetation, degradation of productive land and waterways, and loss of biodiversity, Australia has been judged the worst performer of all the developed countries. Soil problems such as erosion, dryland salinity, acidification in rural areas and shortages of water are now serious and worsening.

None of this is to deny that human development has also had numerous desirable effects. Alan tells us that the explosion of scientific knowledge in recent centuries has underpinned revolutions in health, food production, energy, transport, recreation and communications, as well as producing a host of new consumer goods. Living standards, longevity and household wealth have all been enhanced, especially in developed countries.

It's true, too, as Jeff Sachs reminds us, that many middle-income and rich countries have made progress in controlling *local* pollution—perhaps the aspect of environmental damage most evident to the eyes of citizens. Dirty air and water have been controlled in much of the world. Petrol is now unleaded. Catalytic converters reduce urban smog. Smokestack scrubbers reduce emissions of sulphur dioxide and so limit the problem of acid rain. Even the tough challenge of depletion of the ozone layer has been contained.

But those successes are puny compared with all our other problems. The UN's Millennium Ecosystem Assessment concluded that 'the pressures on ecosystems will increase globally in coming decades unless human attitudes and actions change'. Jeff says that, despite the debate, 'one thing is certain: the current trajectory of human activity is not sustainable'. The distinguished Harvard biologist E.O. Wilson is more forthright in his foreword to Jeff's book: 'The evidence is compelling: we need to redesign our social and economic policies before we wreck this planet.'

Before we go on, it should be clear to you by now that I see merit in much of the environmentalists' critique of the modern world. But that doesn't mean I'm comfortable with all the attitudes adopted by people we think of as 'greenies'. Whereas my kind of environmentalism is based on science, a lot of attitudes expressed under the green banner are anti-scientific: the closed mind on genetically modified food, the embrace of alternative medicine, home birth and even New Age spiritualism. I don't believe everything imported is of the devil. There's a tendency by some to imply that moving to a low-emissions world would involve benefits without costs. Some people who profess the deepest concern about the need to hugely reduce emissions are too quick to rule out nuclear power. And some are overly sceptical about the ability of technological advance to solve environmental problems—especially in the case of carbon capture and storage—except when it comes to renewable energy sources, whose present limitations will be overcome in no time.

The limits to growth

When Donella and Dennis Meadows published their report for the Club of Rome on *The Limits to Growth* in 1972, their contention that the world was running out of certain resources was widely pooh-poohed by economists. Economists argued that, even if it came to pass that supplies of a particular resource—oil, for instance—were close to exhaustion, the imbalance between supply and demand would raise the price of the resource and this would set off a response from the market that would solve the problem. The high price would encourage consumers to economise in their use of the resource and switch to cheaper substitutes. It would encourage suppliers to search for new deposits of the resource and exploit existing deposits that had formerly been uneconomic. It would also create a huge monetary incentive for someone to invent a technological solution to the problem.

From that day to this, few people wishing to be well thought of among economists have dared to suggest there may be limits to the extent that the global economy—or any national economy—can continue expanding, year after year. If the economics profession stands for anything, it's a belief in economic growth. That attitude meets with great approval from business people and most politicians.

There's much truth to the economists' belief in the ability of market forces to respond helpfully to problems such as the proclaimed approach of Peak Oil. And technological advance has eased our way around many more problems in the past than most sceptics seem to realise. Even so, the economists tend to downplay the disruption and difficulties that could beset the economy while we wait for market forces to solve our problems, and in their 'technological optimism' economists do seem close to believing in magic.

I think it's becoming ever more clear that economists will lose the limits-to-growth debate, even though the world economy grew at its fastest ever rate in the years preceding the global financial crisis. Global warming seems an obvious case of the globe being perilously close to reaching one of the limits to growth—including tipping points from which, if they are exceeded, there'll be no return. The conventional approach among economists is to accept the scientists' advice on this, but to believe that if, with the help of 'economic instruments' such as emissions trading schemes or carbon taxes plus copious quantities of new technology, we can make a transition to low-emission sources of energy, then economic growth can continue on its merry way.

I doubt that very much. As I've sought to demonstrate, global warming is just the most obvious and pressing of the limits we face. To climate change we must add the most severe and worsening problems with water, agriculture, fishing and the destruction of species. Can we really expect market forces—even with judicious guidance from 'economic instruments'—to solve our problems on so many fronts and leave us free to continue growing the population, living standards and the economy indefinitely? Can't see it myself.

One factor that's hastened me to this conclusion is the long-established, continuing and remarkably rapid economic growth and development of the world's two most populous countries, China and India. Ignoring ecological limits to growth, there's no definitive reason these countries can't keep growing until their citizens enjoy material standards of living approaching those we in the rich countries have enjoyed for so long. But can those ecological limits be ignored? Is it remotely plausible that the proportion of the world's population consuming resources and energy at the rate we do in Australia could rise from 20 per cent to 60 per cent? Do we have anything like that amount of resources and energy lying idle, waiting to be taken up?

In other words, it's not just where the world is now, it's where the world is showing every sign of wanting to go. There simply aren't enough resources left to go around and I can't believe that 'technology' is capable of magically squaring that circle. The current trajectory of human activity is not sustainable. And the rich world is in no position to advise the poor world to abandon its aspiration to be rich like us. 'Take it from us, being rich isn't all it's cracked up to be.' Such a line would be morally indefensible, not to mention utterly unpersuasive.

The fact that the word 'sustainability' has become such a motherhood sentiment in the public debate is a tacit acknowledgement by most of us that something is going seriously wrong and needs to be changed. But when you consider all the equivocal definitions attached to that word—especially by economists and politicians—you realise there's still a great reluctance to accept its implications.

So what should sustainability mean? It's about the relationship between the present and the future. Reflecting the aforementioned three things the global ecosystem does for the economy, Herman Daly and his colleagues say running a sustainable economy boils down to three simple rules: first, don't use up all the resources; second, don't undermine the delivery of ecological services; and, third, don't overwhelm the waste-absorption capacity.

Elaborating on this elsewhere, Herman says that *renewable* resources (such as timber and fish) must be used at rates not exceeding the rates of regeneration, while non-renewable resources (such as oil and minerals) must be used at rates not exceeding the rate of finding renewable substitutes. The disposal of wastes must not exceed the assimilative capacity of the environment.

In this way, environmental sustainability means not exceeding the world's biophysical 'carrying capacity'—the maximum population size, at a given material standard of living, that can be supported indefinitely without degrading resources. To put it another way, it means living on ecological interest rather than capital so as to maintain the health of the ecosphere. To put it yet another way, it means recognising the need for 'inter-generational equity'—worrying about the state of the world we leave to the next generation.

Does that sound like a tall order? It is. But it's a prescription that accepts the environmental limits to economic growth and doesn't pretend—as so many governments and economists do—that unfettered economic growth remains possible for developed and developing countries alike. Does it sound unfamiliar to you? Is it hard to imagine how we could begin to put such precepts into practice? It is. That's because, however much or little economics you know, all you know is conventional economics, the economics of unfettered growth.

E.O. Wilson says not just that the current trajectory of human activity is unsustainable, but also that we need to redesign our social and economic policies before we wreck this planet. He's right. But where to start? I'd start with a new star to steer by, a new economic model of how the economy works and should work.

Ecological economics

The problem with conventional economics—neoclassical economics—is that it has no place for the environment in its model of how the economy works. This is understandable. When the study of economics started to take a recognisable form more than 200 years ago in the early phases of the Industrial Revolution, economic activity was so small relative to the huge size of the natural world that the services the ecosystem delivered to the economy—including clean air and clean water, but also sinks for emissions of waste—could sensibly be regarded as infinitely available and thus of no great value or importance.

Economics sought to grapple with the problem of 'scarcity': the fact that certain resources—including minerals and energy, but mainly labour and capital equipment—were in limited supply relative to the demand for them because of all the desirable goods and services they could be used to produce. This relative scarcity meant these resources came at a price, and this, in turn, meant they needed to be used with economy and allocated to those uses that delivered most benefit to the community. Such an 'efficient' allocation of resources could be achieved by ensuring the prices of resources reflected their relative scarcity and then allowing market forces to determine the uses to which those resources were put. Economists' role was to study this process and advise governments on what to do—usually, not very much—to ensure markets maximised the community's material wellbeing.

As we've seen, it's really only in recent decades that economic activity has reached sufficient size to threaten the effective functioning of the ecosystem through its excessive demands on both natural resources and waste sinks. And that's left us with a dominant model of the economy with no place for the ecosystem, administered by a profession reluctant to countenance major change and addicted to advocating economic growth above all else.

Because the basic model has no place for the environment and most environmental problems aren't reflected in market prices, those problems—as well as any *favourable* environmental effects—are classed as 'externalities'. They're external to the market system, so special measures have to be taken to incorporate them into the system by 'internalising the externality'.

This is the role of a branch of economics known as *environmental* economics. Environmental economics is, nonetheless, highly conventional—neoclassical—because it focuses on 'economic instruments' aimed at getting the social costs and benefits of environmental issues incorporated into private market prices, then leaving the rest to market forces. The well-known cap-and-trade carbon emissions trading system—as well as its alternative cousin, the carbon tax—is a prime example of the environmental economists' contribution to solving the problem of climate change and their modus operandi.

But the ad hoc attempt to incorporate certain pressing environmental externalities into the market system is a partial and inadequate response to the challenge of ensuring humans' economic activity doesn't collide with the limits of an ever-more overstretched ecosystem. Hence the creation of the far more radical discipline of *ecological* economics by Herman Daly, Robert Costanza and others in the early 1970s. The best concise summary of ecological economics—'the science of sustainability'—comes from the ecologist Robert Goodland's contribution to Herman Daly's festschrift in 2009.

Whereas the focus of environmental economics is on microeconomics (the functioning of particular parts of the economy), the focus of ecological economics is on macro-economics (the functioning of economies as a whole). And to the extent that the earliest economists—Adam Smith, Ricardo, Malthus and John

Stuart Mill—paid more attention to Nature than most contemporary economists, ecological economics is more rooted in classical than neoclassical economics.

Ecological economics constructs a model of the economy that recognises its role as a subsystem nested within the ecosystem and dependent on the ecosystem for its continued healthy functioning. Among many other things, this means the 'resources' with which it is preoccupied are somewhat different from the resources that preoccupy neoclassical economists. In theory, conventional economists focus on 'land, labour and capital', with land covering minerals and other raw materials. In practice, they pay next to no attention to land and raw materials, giving all their attention to labour and, particularly, capital— meaning the man-made capital of buildings, infrastructure and machinery plus, when they think of it, the man-made 'human capital' of education, training and skills.

By contrast, the resources ecological economics focuses on are the natural resources that come from the land—minerals, energy, renewable resources and even water and air. This change of emphasis, Herman explains via his 'compiler' Robert Goodland, merely reflects the way the problem of scarcity has shifted. In the 'empty world' of yore, it made sense to focus on human artefacts because they were in short supply and were the limiting factor for economic activity. There were plenty of fish, for instance, but not enough boats. In today's 'crowded world', however, natural resources are finite and have become scarce. Today, too many boats are chasing too few fish.

Another new dimension of scarcity is the capacity of natural sinks to absorb the waste from our production and consumption of natural resources. This, of course, is what accounts for our problem with climate change. So ecological economics retains economics' traditional preoccupation with 'the problem of scarcity' and its strategy of economising on the limiting factor. But as the problem has shifted from the scarcity of man-made capital to the scarcity of natural capital, so ecological economics has changed the focus.

This explains ecological economics' objection to economic growth: growth means faster extraction and depletion of natural resources and ever more waste to be assimilated by over-stressed sinks, thereby bringing us dangerously close to the ecosystem's natural limits. This leads Herman and his colleagues to draw a sharp distinction between 'growth' and 'development'.

He regards the politicians' 'sustainable growth' as a contradiction in terms, but defines 'sustainable development' as development without growth—that is, without growth in the economy's 'throughput' of natural resources beyond the ecosystem's regenerative and absorptive capacities. Development, on the other hand, involves qualitative improvement in lifestyles, design, technology, efficiency, ordering of priorities and the like.

This brings us to Herman's problem with gross domestic product, the measure of the economy's total production of goods and services during a period, the growth of which conventional economists strive to maximise. Herman says GDP conflates two quite separate things: growth in the throughput of natural resources (which is quantitative and physical) and increases in the efficiency with which resources are used (which is qualitative and non-physical). The point is, of course, that while growth in throughput should be avoided, improvements in efficiency—greater productivity, as defined—are still to be sought.

Implicit in this is that the ecological economists are seeking to move to a 'steady-state' economy: one in which the annual throughput of matter and energy is constant, though its allocation among competing uses is free to vary in response to the market. Herman stresses, however, that the steady state is by no means static. There is continuous renewal by death and birth, depreciation and production, as well as qualitative improvement in the stocks of man-made physical and human capital.

Does the notion of a steady-state economy strike you as way out? Actually, it has a long history in economics. John Stuart Mill wrote in the 19th century that 'a stationary condition of capital and population implies no stationary state of human improvement'. Indeed, there ought to be more likelihood of 'improving the art of living . . . when minds ceased to be engrossed by the art of getting on'. In today's jargon, Mill was arguing for sustainable development—development without growth—that is, qualitative improvement without quantitative increase.

Similarly, Herman and his compiler argue that sustainability is not a new idea in economics, being embedded in the very concept of income. Keynes's great interpreter, Sir John Hicks, defined income as the maximum that can be consumed in a given year without reducing the capacity to produce and consume the same amount next year. So, by definition, income is sustainable consumption. Whatever part of consumption is unsustainable is not income, but the consumption of capital. And the ecological economists want to redraw our national accounts to ensure we don't define as income spending that, in fact, involves dipping into the ecosystem's natural capital. We need to measure progress as living off environmental interest, not environmental capital.

But sustainability can't be our only goal. Our economic goal should be to attain sufficient consumption of resources per person for a good life for all the world's people for a long time. If *present* total resource use is so large it can't be achieved without eating into the earth's capacity to support *future* life in conditions of sufficiency, then it needs to be reduced. Reducing population would help but, failing that, resource use per person should be reduced. Of course, the pain of achieving a decline in total resource use can be reduced to the extent that we can use technological advance to raise the productivity with which we use resources.

Improved productivity in resource use will be slow to happen when resources are priced cheaply. So the first thing to do is remove the various hidden government subsidies of resource prices (such as undercharging for the logging of crown forests, or failing to make trucks pay for the road damage they do). The next thing would be to raise the prices of resources by changing the balance of government revenue-raising from taxing income and capital to taxing resources. Virtually all taxes tend to discourage the activities they are imposed upon, so it makes sense to tax more heavily those activities we wish to discourage than those we don't.

Raising the price of natural resources would encourage greater recycling by making it more economic. It would also be a great spur to businesses to find ways of raising the productivity of their use of those resources. If that was all you did, however, competitive pressures would force the benefit of the productivity gains to be reflected in lower prices. This, in turn, would encourage increased rather than decreased use of resources. The answer is that the use of resources would also need quantitative restrictions similar to the slowly lowering cap (upper limit) on emissions used in cap-and-trade emissions trading schemes. Such restrictions would keep the prices of natural resources high notwithstanding improvements in the productivity of their use.

Conventional economists wrestle with the two, often-conflicting goals of promoting efficiency and promoting fairness (equity). This would also be the case under the ecological economists' model. They would continue to rely on prices and market competition to achieve the most efficient allocation of resources. But markets can't be relied on to achieve a just distribution of income between the rich and poor, as most conventional economists accept. So governments have to intervene to redistribute income from the rich to the poor, and achieving a just distribution would be all the more important in a steady-state economy where the government was deliberately raising the prices of energy and other natural resources, and quite possibly exerting downward pressure on material living standards.

But that leaves a third key variable, 'scale', which is missing from the concerns of conventional economists but is crucial to the achievement of sustainable development. Because they see no impediment to the pursuit of unending economic growth—including continuing growth in the throughput of natural resources—conventional economists see no reason to worry about the scale of economic activity relative to the ecosystem's ability to cope with that activity.

By contrast, ensuring the physical scale of economic activity stays within—or returns to—the limits imposed by the ecosystem is the whole point of the ecological economists' model. Again, the acceptable scale of activity can't be left to the market, but has to be imposed on the market by the government, with the price mechanism left to achieve an efficient allocation of resources within the constraint imposed by the government.

Herman says what needs to be added to the working of the economy is the equivalent of a Plimsoll line—the line that's painted around the hull of a boat. When the boat sinks in the water below the Plimsoll line it's readily apparent that it's been dangerously overloaded. The economic Plimsoll line, the upper limits to be set on the annual use of natural resources—whether in total or with separate limits for particular resources—would be imposed by the government following guidance from leading scientists, just as the targets for the reduction of greenhouse gas emissions are (or should be) based on the advice of special committees of the world's top climate scientists.

The final issue for the ecological economists to grapple with is the yawning divide between the rich countries and the poor countries, and the latter's understandable, indeed insistent, aspirations to material standards of living even remotely approaching those enjoyed for so long by the developed countries. Can it be the same regime for both the developed and the developing worlds? Hardly. That would be neither fair nor realistic.

Herman says that, though both sides need to put a lot more effort into limiting population growth, the developed countries should put more emphasis on controlling overconsumption, while the developing countries should focus more on population. Why should the poor control their population if the resources saved thereby are merely gobbled up by the rich's overconsumption? But, by the same token, why should the rich control their overconsumption if the saved resources merely allow a larger number of poor people to subsist at the same level of misery?

Does all this strike you as hopelessly unrealistic politically? Controlling population growth is daunting enough, but what politician would dare advocate reducing overconsumption? Perhaps at present it is unrealistic. But, in the end, politicians are followers of public opinion more than leaders of it. And, unless the great weight of scientific opinion is wildly astray, the mismatch between economic activity and the Earth's carrying capacity will only become more pressing, with more day-to-day evidence of the harm our excesses are doing to the environment *and* our formerly cosy way of life.

The will to do what needs to be done to avert catastrophe *is* missing at present. Perhaps we need to run closer to the precipice before that will materialises. But if so, it's as well for the more prescient among us to have started thinking about what will need to be done.

9

TOWARDS THE HAPPY SOCIETY

In economics exams the questions don't change from
one decade to the next, but the answers do.
— Economists' saying

We live in a more materialistic age and we've all been caught
up to a greater or lesser extent. But if the science of
happiness teaches us anything it's that materialism isn't all it's
cracked up to be. It's not that we should be living like paupers,
but that we're forever pursuing money and the things it buys at
the expense of the less alluring but ultimately more satisfying
aspects of our lives, such as our relationships with family, friends
and neighbours.

One telling indicator of our greater materialism is our choice
to take the benefits of the increased productivity of our labour
in the form of higher wages rather than more hours of leisure.
The governments we elect—of both colours—not only reflect
our increased materialism, they actively promote it. In the politicians' lexicon, 'aspirational' is a euphemism for materialistic.
Another euphemism for our thirst for ever more and bigger
and better possessions is that great idol to which almost all
politicians genuflect, 'economic growth'.

It's obviously every individual's right to decide whether and in what way they'll pursue happiness. I don't doubt that everyone does. You may be devoted to duty, beauty, academic inquiry or even ambition and self-aggrandisement, but surely these are just different attempted paths to happiness—or satisfaction, if you prefer. After all, whose goal is to be unhappy?

But whereas no one doubts the individual's right to pursue happiness, many question whether the pursuit of national happiness is an appropriate goal for governments. I don't. I think governments have long been in the happiness business—as they should be. They don't use the word and they may not think of it that way, but that doesn't change the reality.

Many economists would see it as government's role to maximise 'social welfare'. And every pollie would happily confess to pursuing economic growth. But why? Where's that supposed to get us? It's supposed to advance our national well-being. And what's that if not our collective happiness? The point is not that our governments haven't been seeking to increase our happiness, it's that they haven't been going about it the right way—just as so many of us as individuals have been barking up the wrong trees.

De-throning the god of growth

After decades of thinking and writing about economics and what it's supposed to bring us, I've finally come to the conclusion that economists are mistaken in their advocacy of unending economic growth. Admittedly, our quest for greater affluence has brought us many benefits—longer, healthier and far more comfortable lives—but the rich countries have reached the point where the visible benefits of affluence are close to being exceeded by the less-visible costs, if we haven't already passed it.

This book has made this point at the level of the individual's search for happiness and at the level of the way we manage our society. The material dimension is inescapably important, but we've fallen into the trap of valuing it too highly and this has crowded out other, less-tangible aspects of our life. We need to switch the focus from the quantity of consumption to the quality of life.

Undoubtedly, the most powerful and pressing argument against the rich countries' continued pursuit of economic growth is ecological. As I argued in detail in Chapter 8, humans' ever-increasing use of natural resources and generation of waste are perilously close to exceeding the ecosystem's capacity to absorb without serious impairment. Greenhouse gas emissions and global warming may be the area where we're closest to passing the point of no return, but our threat to the ecosystem—and hence to our present comfortable way of life—is growing on many other fronts: to fish stocks, forests, the availability of water, agriculture and the survival of species.

The need for the affluent countries to revise their attitude to growth is made all the more pressing by the rapid economic and population growth of the developing world, led by China and India. I find it inconceivable that sufficient natural resources exist to permit the almost 40 per cent of the world's population represented by China and India to reach material living standards even remotely approaching those we in the rich countries have enjoyed for so long. And then there's the question of whether the ecosystem could cope with all the additional wastes and emissions.

There's no way we can deter the world's poor from continuing to use rapid economic growth to pursue higher material living standards—and no moral basis on which we could urge them to do as we say, not as we do. So, quite apart from our desire for self-preservation in avoiding ecological catastrophe, the case against growth is a moral imperative: we must stop growing so as to leave room for the poor countries to continue growing. Although in our pursuit of materialism we've reached the point of greatly diminished—perhaps even negative—returns, they haven't.

Keep in mind as I criticise 'growth' in this chapter, I'm using the word as shorthand. As we saw in Chapter 8, it's growth in the throughput of natural resources we should forswear, not the rise in gross domestic product that comes from the continued pursuit of productivity improvement.

So far in enumerating the reasons for ceasing to promote growth we've covered environmental self-preservation and moral obligation. Now we come to the burden of this book, which is more self-interested and pragmatic: past a certain point, economic growth doesn't work anyway. It doesn't live up to its billing; we—and our politicians, economists and business people—confidently believe that greater production and consumption of goods and services will make us happier, but the scientific study of happiness tells us it doesn't.

As we saw in Chapter 4, the doubling or trebling in real income per person in developed countries over the past four or five decades has been accompanied by no appreciable increase in nation-wide measures of subjective wellbeing. Research by psychologists and some economists suggests there are two main reasons for this. First, the human capacity for adaptation, where a pay rise, for instance, might make us happier at first, but we quickly become used to it and build it into our definition of normal. Second, our tendency to compare ourselves with others.

To put it the way an economist would, it's only increases in our *relative* income that are likely to make us happier, not increases in our absolute income. And the trouble with this is that while some people can increase their relative income, not everyone can. Indeed, all those individuals who gain by moving ahead in the pecking order should be offset by all those who lose by being pushed back in the order.

This is bad news for all those who believe that governments' promotion of economic growth can make us happier. Governments can increase incomes generally—and their efforts may increase some people's incomes more than others—but, obviously, they can't increase everyone's relative income. And their continued efforts to raise incomes in general serve only to promote a kind of status arms race in which many of us strive to increase our social standing by using our higher incomes to buy those things that impress people, without this contest doing anything to raise the wellbeing of the community as a whole.

Because our basic needs for food, clothing, shelter and a modest degree of comfort were satisfied a long time ago, it's likely that much of our increased spending as our real incomes have kept rising over the years has gone on the purchase of 'positional goods'—goods or services designed to display to others our superior position in the pecking order. Spending on things such as designer-label clothes and accessories, flash restaurants (my own specialty), better located and better appointed homes, imported cars, private schools for the kids, and so on.

Defenders of growth sometimes argue that even if it's true that higher material living standards do nothing to raise the community's *subjective* wellbeing they certainly raise our *objective* wellbeing, so why not persist with growth? Well, the first answer is present in the question. To the extent that our increased incomes are being devoted to status competition, this is socially wasteful. From a nation-wide perspective, a lot of resources and human effort are being expended on activity that yields no overall gain. And for this to be happening at a time when the global economy are at risk of exceeding its ecological limits and when we may be crowding out the more legitimate material aspirations of the developing countries makes it even harder to defend.

As we saw in Chapter 7, the economists' conventional way of thinking about and measuring economic growth ignores the costs it generates, creating the misperception that growth is a free lunch (and we know what economists have warned us about those). This is mainly because the costs occur outside the market system. Apart from the (considerable) costs imposed on the natural environment, this is mainly because those costs are non-material and non-monetary, thus making them hard to see and hard to measure. (It's also likely that, at the time when economic methodology was being laid down, these costs were a lot smaller and less evident.)

This being the case, it's hard for the critics of growth to reel off a lot of facts and figures revealing the size and significance of those costs. If we weren't so mesmerised by growth we might have put more effort into trying to measure the downside. Even so, it does seem clear that our economic growth, the drive for greater efficiency in the allocation of resources and the 'marketisation' of more aspects of daily life have claimed a price in terms of damage to family life and broader social relationships, reduced job security and satisfaction, and increased uncertainty, instability and stress. The spread of the market has made social relationships more impersonal, unthinkingly weakening valuable social norms, eroding trust and loyalty, and thereby eating into social capital and diminishing feelings of being part of a caring community.

At the level of the individual, heightened materialism means spending long hours working for the income that allows us to buy more stuff, at the expense of relationships with family and friends, recreation (better read as *re-creation*) and possibly health. At the level of public policies to promote growth, we have a lot of workers displaced from their jobs and not a lot of effort to help them find another. We have the growing commercialisation of the weekend, with all its disruption to the family lives of people required to work.

But where would the jobs come from?

There's a common belief that you and I have little choice but to keep spending to keep the wheels of the capitalist economy turning over and stop it collapsing in a heap. That's true—up to a point. But the plain fact is that it wouldn't be possible for all of us to stop spending, nor is anyone suggesting we should. What's in debate is not whether we should junk our economy but whether it needs to keep getting bigger year after year (and whether we should regard the continuation and size of that growth as the ultimate sign of progress).

A better objection is: but don't we need continued growth in our economy to create the additional jobs for our ever-growing workforce? To me, this is the main stumbling block involved in any move to a 'steady-state' economy. But it could be overcome. For a start, more than half Australia's growth in population—and, more pertinently, our population of working age—comes from net immigration. Since it's debat-able whether, overall, the immigrants do all that much to add to GDP *per person*—whether they make the existing population better off, as opposed to merely making the economy bigger—we could reduce the size of the problem by slashing our immigration program. (As an aside, this would significantly reduce the upward pressure on house prices, as well as making it much easier for us to reduce our greenhouse gas emissions. It would also reduce the *world's* emissions because the emissions of the average immigrant are about double what they would have been back home.)

At a time when we're starting to worry about shortages of labour arising from the ageing of the population—more old people retiring from the workforce than young people joining it—the question of where the jobs would come from is obviously less pressing than it would have been in the past.

But one policy that would help is for governments to encourage or require the benefit from improvements in the productivity of labour to be taken as reductions in working hours rather than increases in real wage rates. (This would have the additional benefit of helping to reduce the growth in consumer spending.) And failing that, governments could do more to encourage job sharing.

While we're on the subject of employment, although economists and politicians frequently cite increasing job opportunities as one of the great advantages of economic growth, in truth the object of the neoclassical exercise is increasing the material standard of living, not reducing unemployment. That the pursuit of greater affluence leads to increased employment is just a fortunate by-product.

This helps explain why economists are usually unenthusiastic about using job sharing to reduce unemployment. Why cut jobs in half when by revving up the economy you can greatly increase the demand for labour? The little-trumpeted truth is that the economists' neoclassical model—which pervades their thinking more than most of them realise—*assumes* the economy is in a continuous state of full employment. This shows why their model is always telling them that 'reforms' involving the displacement of workers would be an unalloyed boon to the nation.

Life in the steady-state gulag

I've always been excited and challenged by the notion that conventional economics has been overtaken by advances in other sciences, by changes in the world and even by capitalism's success in overcoming scarcity, and is thus in need of its own reform. Wow. What changes would we need to make to produce a new model better suited to the problems of the 21st century? What would have to go and what could stay?

But I've met few economists who share that excitement. It seems clear from their defensiveness and the speed and vehemence with which they reject the arguments against continued economic growth that they find the idea threatening. Well, it may be a threat to their long-internalised view of the world and perhaps to some part of their intellectual capital, but of one thing you can be sure: it's not a threat to their jobs. Were we and our political leaders to decide we wanted to end the pursuit of growth, we'd need lots of economists to figure out how such an economy could be made to work and how the transition from growth to steady-state could be managed without mishap.

Part of the problem is also, I suspect, a lack of imagination. There's a temptation on the part of economists—and others— to envisage an economy not motivated by the pursuit of growth as like something out of East Berlin. No advertising or consumer choice to brighten up the place, no reason to try. And with everyone sitting round being happy, where would the progress come from?

A steady-state economy wouldn't be nearly as drab or inert as the doubters fear. For a start, we're talking about a switch of emphasis—a change in the definition of success—from quantity to quality, from growth to development. Progress would mean getting better, not getting bigger. As we saw in Chapter 8, growth in productivity would still be pursued provided it didn't involve increased use of natural resources.

It's a mistake to imagine that government's adoption of increased subjective wellbeing as its overarching objective would involve people doing little but having a good time. As we saw from the outset, any sensible definition of happiness involves more than the pursuit of pleasure, thus leaving plenty of room for striving—to build a better mousetrap or make the world a better place in other ways. You'd like to be at the forefront of the search for a cancer cure? No one's going to stop you.

It's another instance of model blindness to imagine that, without growth in natural resource use, no one would have a motive for trying hard. Humans are motivated by a host of desires apart from money: power, status, distinction, job satisfaction, intrinsic interest in the subject, loyalty and duty. The human animal is innately restless and inquisitive. Nothing's going to change that.

Similarly, humans are innately competitive, particularly men. The notion that they have to be bribed to compete is a fiction spread by greedy chief executives. Even so, with less monetary force feeding of our competitive instinct, it's possible we could see more co-operative behaviour, which would be no bad thing. Humans are also innately co-operative and social.

Too often under our present arrangements, growth serves as a substitute for improvement. That's particularly evident in business leaders' pursuit of progress by takeover. It's common for company takeovers to fail to increase the success of the merged entity, yet the sharemarket's enthusiasm for takeovers remains undiminished. Takeovers would still be possible in a steady-state economy, of course, since they don't involve growth in the overall market. But at a broader level it's possible that when the pursuit of bigness was discouraged, there'd be increased emphasis on productivity improvement.

Moving to a no-growth world would change the constraints on the economy and alter the object of the exercise without removing the need for a (much improved) model of how that world would work or the expert advice of economists. Nor would it eliminate the need for day-to-day management of the macro economy.

Macro-economic management—aimed at smoothing out the ups and downs in the business cycle—would continue to have a vital role to play in any move to make maximising 'aggregate happiness' the explicit goal of government policy. That's because happiness research has revealed the importance to people's subjective wellbeing of the opposing evils of macro management: inflation and unemployment.

Both inflation and unemployment reduce people's happiness although, not surprisingly, unemployment worries people a lot more than inflation does. So, yes, the macro manager's efforts to keep the economy on a reasonably even keel, thus avoiding significant worsening in either inflation or unemployment, remain a high priority in a more happiness-conscious world. It's possible, however, that in an economy where less was done to encourage growth, the swings in the business cycle would be much smaller.

How the absence of growth would foster wellbeing

So much for why the absence of economic growth wouldn't be the desert that many people fear, but what about actual benefits? Apart from helping to avert ecological calamity, how would it add to happiness? Many of the things that reduce our happiness stem from the search for greater efficiency so as to contribute to economic growth. Easing the efficiency imperative would be hugely liberating. It would reduce the push for a lot of things that diminish happiness. For one thing, it could greatly improve employers' treatment of their workers, but that's such a big topic we'll deal with it under its own heading.

Less emphasis on efficiency might halt the trend by governments and businesses to spread the market to new aspects of our lives. As we saw in Chapter 7, this often does increase efficiency, but it does so by making relations more impersonal and thus reducing the quiet satisfaction that comes from reciprocity in social relations.

Similarly, many efforts to increase efficiency have the unintended and often unnoticed side effect of eroding social capital—such as trust and norms of acceptable behaviour—and reducing our sense of community. For instance, efficiency is enhanced by a high degree of geographic mobility of labour—workers moving freely to locations where their labour is in greater demand—which sounds great until you remember the way it breaks up extended families, separating young mothers from their own mothers and adult children from their aged parents. A little less efficiency and a little more human contact could greatly increase happiness.

Less emphasis on growth and efficiency could make employers less keen to urge their workers to put in long hours and make it easier for governments to see the social benefits of leisure. The length of annual leave could be increased—four weeks a year is not high by European standards—the pressure to reduce public holidays and separate them from the weekend could be resisted, and a rear-guard action fought to prevent any further incursions into the weekend. Perhaps the efforts to halt growth in consumption could involve reintroducing restrictions on shopping hours.

Many of the measures governments could take to discourage economic growth would have upsides for the happiness of individuals. Advertising is a good case in point. Advertising must cause consumption to be higher than otherwise—why else would businesses spend so much on it?—so governments could be expected to take steps to limit it. We could expect this to lead to a decline in 'buyer's remorse'—regretting decisions to buy things. But much advertising, particularly on television and product-placement in movies, works by making us dissatisfied with our lot—why can't my life be more glamorous, less stressed and more loving like those people on the screen?—and making an implied promise to satisfy the need it has created. There'd be less dissatisfaction in the world if there was less advertising.

In their efforts to discourage growth, governments could be expected to discourage socially wasteful spending on status-signalling 'positional goods'. They could do this by taxing their consumption more heavily than the consumption of non-positional goods. Or they might increase their own spending on non-positional goods, many of which are best supplied by governments.

Holidays are non-positional—your friends and neighbours can't see what you do when you go away—but research suggests they generate more satisfaction than buying fancy stuff your friends *can* see. Surveys show that time spent commuting is often the least happy period in people's day. Increased government spending on public transport, perhaps motivated by a desire to reduce energy use and carbon emissions, could reduce unhappiness at the same time (not to mention reducing upward pressure on the prices of homes closer to the centre of the city). Government spending to reduce water, air and noise pollution is another non-positional good, and such pollution does a lot to reduce the happiness of people in affected areas.

Surveys of subjective wellbeing demonstrate something economists have never before known whether to believe in: that thanks to diminishing marginal utility, an extra $1000 of annual income adds far less to the happiness of the well-off than it does to the happiness of people on low incomes. So using tax and government spending to redistribute income from the well-off to the less well-off should increase total wellbeing. And, indeed, wellbeing surveys confirm that, for most developed countries bar the United States, those with a narrower gap between rich and poor tend to be happier.

Governments that adopt a no-growth strategy are likely to want to do more redistribution of income, especially if measures to increase the tax on the use of natural resources while reducing the tax on income hit low income-earners disproportionately. Now, economists often use the case of income redistribution in defence of economic growth, arguing that it leads to much less resistance if you change the size of the slices at a time when the cake itself is getting bigger.

This ought to be a good argument. But we've seen the size of the cake grow a lot in recent decades without seeing much evidence of governments seizing the opportunity to quietly redistribute cake in favour of people on lower incomes. If anything, we've seen the reverse. Why have politicians been cutting income tax more at the top than in the middle or lower down? They've done it in the name of increasing the incentive for top people to work harder—to promote economic efficiency, in other words.

So, sorry, I'm not buying the growing-cake argument. I think it's just as plausible to argue that, if in a no-growth world we could douse the fires of materialist aspiration—if we could change the prevailing ethic that greed is good—the better-off might calm down and be less resistant to the claims of those less well-off than themselves. If so, we could expect total happiness to increase.

Here's a benefit that would arise not so much from abandoning the growth objective as from recognising that humans aren't the clear-headed rational calculators the economists' model assumes. Governments would accept that their citizens often have trouble controlling their desires for things with immediate attractions but long-term costs—junk food, alcohol, television, gambling, credit, and all the rest. They'd understand that people commonly set up 'commitment devices' to help keep their urges under control, and that this is a good thing which ought to be encouraged and, in some cases, actively facilitated.

Sometimes, however, the best solution is for governments to remove or reduce temptation by outlawing certain practices (speeding, for instance) or enticements (cigarette advertising). A more up-to-date and scientific understanding of human motivation would disabuse governments of the notion that the individual always knows best and would always object to having their freedom limited. On the contrary, people often appreciate governments taking temptation out of their way because they know how unsuccessful struggles against temptation make them unhappy.

As we've seen, a no-growth economy wouldn't be an economy without change. Change is inevitable, and life might be pretty deadly without it—though that's often a judgement made in hindsight rather than at the time. (When I was growing up in the supposedly terminally boring fifties, they seemed pretty good to me.) It's reasonable to expect, however, that with less growth for the sake of growth there'd be less change for the sake of change. And it has to be acknowledged that, even if it makes the world a better place in some way, incessant, externally imposed change generates a lot of unhappiness for a lot of people, even if they eventually adjust to their changed circumstances.

The one fear I have in all this concerns micro-economic reform. At its best, micro reform aims at rolling back entrenched economic privilege awarded in times past to certain industries to protect them from disruption and decline at the hands of external influences. The trouble is that you can only protect the firms and workers in particular industries at the expense of all the firms and workers in the unprotected industries.

The motive for unwinding these protections—which is always bitterly resisted—is the desire to improve the efficiency with which the economy's resources are allocated, thereby adding to economic growth to the (material) benefit of the rest of the economy. My fear is that, were the goal of increased efficiency to be abandoned, the motive for rolling back areas of privilege would be lost. It would then be a matter of first in, best dressed. Workers in unprotected industries would be obliged to continue propping up protected industries in perpetuity, with a great likelihood that, should further difficult times emerge, the privileged industries would be first in line for additional assistance in the name of preserving the status quo.

Were the lack of concern about efficiency to lead to protection for a lot more industries under pressure, we could end up staunchly defending an industrial museum against all pressure for change. It seems clear from this that concern about efficiency in the allocation of resources can't just be tossed out the window. Rather, governments need to adopt a more balanced approach, weighing the material benefits of great efficiency against the psychic costs and, when it comes to proposals to increase happiness, weighing the psychic benefits against the material costs of reduced efficiency.

And here's a point for the economists to ponder. As we saw in Chapter 5, while it wouldn't be surprising to be told that successful people tend to be happier, more sophisticated research that seeks to establish the 'direction of causation' is showing it also works the other way: happier people tend to be more successful, to be healthier, have better relationships and be more successful in their jobs and more highly paid. So the more governments do to permit people to be happier—or to reduce the incidence of ill-being—the more they'll help people to be the way economists think they should be.

Small is beautiful, local is likeable

A lot of the push for ever-greater efficiency involves the pursuit of economies of scale in the production of goods and services. And, indeed, a lot of the increase in our material standard of living over the centuries is owed to our efforts to increase the scale of production. Similarly, there are benefits in having banks and businesses operating on a nation-wide level gathering people's savings and deciding where around the nation that money should be reinvested. To put it another way, it's less risky for the people in a particular region if they don't have all their savings invested in that region.

But when it comes to our feelings of competence, connectedness and autonomy—feelings that have a great influence over our happiness—it's not at all clear that bigger is better. Indeed, quite the reverse. As Alain de Botton has wisely said, 'large-scale is meaning-inefficient'. One of the big problems with the modern world—with the ordinary person's understanding of how the economy works and governments work—is that it's become so hugely complicated we can no longer see the links, see what causes what.

Complexity—the inability of anyone but the experts to understand how things work—can make systems dysfunctional. It's also disempowering and isolating. Note, too, that not all the costs of bigness are psychological. When organisations get too big, the economies of scale can be outweighed by the diseconomies of scale, such as the greater difficulty of communication between so many people in differing locations and avoiding duplication of effort—a much under-recognised phenomenon, which often plays a big part in causing business and government amalgamations to be far less beneficial in practice than they look on paper.

By contrast, one of the great advantages of working for a small business is that everything's on a comprehensible scale. You know how the business works and who does what. You know your boss and your boss knows you. You know how hard your boss works and your boss knows how hard you work. If you take a day off work, your boss knows why. When your boss judges your performance, it is done so knowing all your strengths and weakness, not by reading a number on a computer printout. If your boss wants to lay you off or sack you, this has to be done to your face and with a very clear idea of how much difficulty it will create for you. Your boss can't hide behind the anonymity of a big organisation.

Australia's two big retailers, Woolworths and Wesfamers/ Coles, dominate supermarkets, are big in department stores, have bought out or forced out many independent liquor stores, are now fighting it out in hardware retailing and would just love to be allowed into pharmacy. Most people look at this and worry about 'market power'. Are the Big Two using the reduced number of their competitors to overcharge customers—or underpay small suppliers—and fatten their own profits?

These are standard economic efficiency concerns. But there's another way of looking at the issue: when you're obliged to switch from dealing with a small local firm, with a shopkeeper you know, to dealing with a huge, impersonal national retail chain, is there a loss of satisfaction from that change? Is it adequately compensated for by the likelihood that the chain's prices are lower?

I don't find it hard to accept there is a barely identified loss of subjective wellbeing when our buying and selling becomes more impersonal. If governments were less preoccupied with promoting growth, they could do more to inhibit the duopolisation of markets—two seems to be the natural number for concentration in an economy of our size—to preserve a role for smaller players just for the sake of smallness. This would probably come at some small cost to economic efficiency, but in a more enlightened, more balanced world it could be seen as a small price to pay.

The principle of 'subsidiarity' states that matters should be handled at the least centralised level that makes sense. If reduced concern about growth and bigness led governments and businesses to see the often subtle benefits of 'localism', that would strike a blow for greater happiness. There may be losses of scale economies, but these can be outweighed by the benefits (including the avoidance of diseconomies of scale).

I think there could be much to be gained—in terms of both feelings of community and genuine efficiency in achieving the organisation's stated purpose—by allowing schools and hospitals to be managed by local boards. More controversially, I see psychic advantages in encouraging more of a town or region's transactions to be made with local firms and more of its savings to be reinvested locally. The advantages are a greater ability to trace through chains of cause and effect, feelings of belonging, feelings of being able to determine your own future and the security that reciprocal obligation brings. In short, localism brings things down to a human scale.

Bendigo Bank has done well from its strategy of offering suburbs and towns a mixture of local solidarity and participation in a reasonable-sized national network. If localism is to flourish, governments will need to work on devices that permit local concentration while reducing the risk of local institutions pulling each other down in the event of a local setback.

A new realm of job enhancement

If governments were to make maximising people's subjective wellbeing their highest priority rather than maximising living standards, you'd expect them to place a lot more emphasis on increasing the satisfaction workers get from their jobs. We spend so much of our lives working that making work more satisfying ought to be a high priority. The neoclassical model's assumption that people work solely for the money it brings defies common experience. And research into happiness strongly confirms that much of the happiness workers feel comes from their jobs. Work is a source of intrinsic satisfaction—people enjoy it for its own sake—and this insight needs to fully inform governments' policies on the labour market and industrial relations. Helping to improve people's work experience is such an obvious way to increase happiness.

At the level of individual businesses, if we could get away from the notion that bigger is always better and growth is the key sign of success as a leader, attitudes towards employees could be radically different. I'd like to see advancing the wellbeing of employees raised to be an objective at least equal to the interests of shareholders and customers.

Not possible because company law requires primacy to be given to shareholders' interests? That's the popular cant, but don't believe it. It's been a legal requirement since early times, but chief executives have been preaching sermons about it only in recent times. And, as we all know, in truth they give highest priority to advancing their own remuneration. No, in reality, the objectives of big business are determined by the social norms of behaviour prevailing among executives at the time. So if they wanted to upgrade the priority of employee welfare they could.

What would do most to increase happiness is to 'enhance' jobs—make them more attractive and satisfying. How? Well, first, firms need to change their attitudes towards employee rewards. It's simply wrong to imagine that offers of more money are the only or even the main way to encourage greater effort and commitment. That may hold for senior executives, but not for lesser mortals.

Wide discrepancies in the pay of people in similar job categories can do more to create dissatisfaction than to motivate individuals, although the establishment of career paths, where workers receive known increments for doing more skilled work or accepting more responsibility, can deliver motivation and satisfaction.

But if money isn't the key to satisfaction and job enhancement, what is? Job design. Workers are happiest when their jobs meet their human need for competence, relatedness and autonomy. Competence means our ability to control our environment and experience ourselves as capable and effective. Relatedness means a sense of belonging, being connected to others and treated as a respected member of the group. Autonomy means organising your own actions and the experience of being causal—making a difference. Putting it another way, humans are both working animals and social animals; they see themselves as both individuals and part of a group.

Individuals need to fit the jobs they're given and jobs need to be designed to fit the individual typical to that kind of employment. Workers on production lines get less bored when they're moved to different tasks. Semi-autonomous work groups can perform well and be highly satisfying to their members. Skilled white-collar employees, particularly those who work on successive projects, can be given increased flexibility to choose their working times. 'If you meet the deadline and do a good job, I don't care when you work.'

None of this means turning the workplace into a Sunday school where all is sweetness and light. Life can get pretty tough for individuals who let down the other members of their work group. A good job involves a fair degree of challenge—so long as it's challenge the worker has the ability to meet (see individuals fitting the jobs they're given). Even periods of stress are fine—say, in the run-up to deadlines, rather than from perpetually unreasonable bosses. Most workers are happy to give it extra when they've internalised the organisation's objectives. Most workers *want* to be loyal to their employer—it makes them feel good—it's just that they want loyalty coming back the other way. Like all humans they have a deep belief in reciprocity.

Happy, satisfied workers are better workers. They're likely to experience fewer personal problems, such as marital discord or alcohol abuse, as well as being healthier. That equals less absenteeism. They're inclined to be more creative. They're good organisational citizens. So a happy workforce should have higher productivity. Certainly, workers should have a lower rate of turnover and so generate lower recruitment costs. They can give a good employer an advantage over his competitors.

Where too few employers see the wisdom of giving their employees a better deal, governments could become more daring in outlawing damaging work practices. To mention just a couple of personal bugbears, shift work is bad enough in interfering with the body's circadian rhythm, but rolling shift work—where you move through a sequence of day shift, afternoon shift and night shift—is clearly injurious to the health. Split shifts—where you work the morning peak, clock off for a few hours and come back for the afternoon peak—are an unreasonable intrusion on employees' free time because there's so little they can do during the break apart from hanging around.

All these enhancements would benefit women as well as men. But women need more than that. The rising level of women's educational attainment—to the point where it equals or exceeds that for men—has helped us see how much the institutions and social norms of the workforce have developed over the centuries to accommodate the needs of men. Those institutions need to be reformed to better accommodate the needs of women, particularly mothers. This makes sense even from the narrowest, most growth-obsessed perspective. The taxpayer, parents and the women themselves have gone to great trouble and expense to educate women; those women want to exercise their skills in the workforce and it's simply wasteful to fail to break down the barriers to their full participation. From a happiness perspective, we all know the frustration and stress many women experience in juggling work and family.

Improvements in the provision of affordable childcare and the introduction of paid parental leave are big steps forward, but more remains to be done. Paradoxically to some, this includes breaking down the employer attitudes that inhibit fathers from playing a bigger part in the care of their children. Where employers are slow to see the logic of doing more to accommodate women's needs, governments are justified in imposing solutions.

The take-away

Governments' stated policy objective is to promote the wellbeing of their citizens, but they need a broader and more balanced conception of wellbeing, one that goes beyond increasing our material standard of living and that benefits from recent advances in science, particularly in psychology and ecology. Objective wellbeing is important, but so too is subjective wellbeing. The difference between the reality and the perception is more significant than those of us educated in the rationalist ethos are schooled to appreciate. If certain actions make us better off materially but make us feel worse, the cause of that discrepancy needs to be identified and responded to. In the end, we are what we feel.

BIBLIOGRAPHY

Argyle, Michael (1999) 'Causes and Correlates of Happiness' in *Well-Being: The Foundations of Hedonic Psychology*, Russell Sage Foundation, New York.

—— (2001) *The Psychology of Happiness*, 2nd edn, Routledge, Hove.

Ashcroft, John and Caroe, Phil (2007) *Thriving Lives: Which Way for Well-being?*, Relationships Foundation, Cambridge.

Australian Unity (2008) *What makes us happy?*, Australian Unity Wellbeing Index, Melbourne.

Ben-Ami, Daniel (2006) 'Who's happiest: Denmark or Vanuatu?', www.spiked-online.com, 7 August.

Blanchflower, David and Oswald, Andrew (2007) 'Is wellbeing U-shaped over the life cycle?', National Bureau of Economic Research working paper no. 12935, Cambridge, MA.

Brooks, Arthur C. (2008) *Gross National Happiness*, Basic Books, New York.

Camerer, Colin, Loewenstein, George and Prelec, Drazen (2005) 'Neuroeconomics: How neuroscience can inform economics', *Journal of Economic Literature*, vol. XLIII, March, pp. 9–64.

Caroll, Christopher (1998) 'Why do the rich save so much?', National Bureau of Economic Research working paper no. W6549, Cambridge, MA.

Cosmides, Leda and Tooby, John, www.psych.ucsb.edu/research/cep/primer.html, accessed December 2009.

Csikszentmihalyi, Mihaly (1990) *Flow: The Psychology of Optimal Experience*, Harper Perennial, New York.

Daly, Herman (1996) *Beyond Growth*, Beacon Press, Boston.

De Botton, Alain (2009) *The Pleasures and Sorrows of Work*, Hamish Hamilton, London.

Di Tella, Rafael, Haisken-De New, John and MacCulloch, Robert (2007) 'Happiness Adaptation to Income and to Status in an Individual Panel', National Bureau of Economic Research working paper no. 13159, Cambridge, MA.

Diener, Ed and Biswas-Diener, Robert (2008) *Happiness: Unlocking the Mysteries of Psychological Wealth*, Blackwell, Malden.

Dunn, Elizabeth, Aknin, Lara and Norton, Michael (2008) 'Spending money on others promotes happiness', *Science*, vol. 319, pp. 1687–8.

Easterlin, Richard (1974) 'Does income growth improve the human lot? Some empirical evidence' reprinted in *Happiness and Economics* (2002), Richard Easterlin and Edward Elgar (eds), Cheltenham.

—— (2005) 'Building a better theory of well-being' in *Economics & Happiness*, Luigino Bruni and Pier Luigi Porta (eds), Oxford University Press, Oxford.

Evans, Dylan and Selina, Howard (2001) *Introducing Evolution*, Icon Books, Royston.

Frank, Robert H. (1999) *Luxury Fever*, The Free Press, New York.

Frey, Bruno (2008) *Happiness: A Revolution in Economics*, MIT Press, Cambridge, MA.

Frey, Bruno S. and Stutzer, Alois (2002) *Happiness and Economics*, Princeton University Press, Princeton.

Gilbert, Daniel (2004) www.edge.org/3rd_culture/gilbert03/gilbert_index.html, accessed October 2009.

—— (2006) *Stumbling on Happiness*, Alfred A. Knopf, New York.

Goodland, Robert (2009) 'Herman Daly Festschrift', www.eoearth.org/article/Herman_Daly_Festschrift~_The_w

orld_is_in_overshoot_and_what_to_do_about_it, accessed October 2009.

Haidt, Jonathan (2006) *The Happiness Hypothesis*, Basic Books, New York.

Hamilton, Clive (2003) *Growth Fetish*, Allen & Unwin, Sydney.

Hirsch, Fred (1976) *Social Limits to Growth*, Harvard University Press, Cambridge, MA.

Huxley, Aldous (1932) *Brave New World*, Chatto and Windus, London.

Iaffaldano, Michelle and Muchinsky, Paul (1985) 'Job satisfaction and job performance: A meta-analysis', *Psychological Bulletin*, vol. 97, no. 2.

Jones, A.R. (2007) 'Homo sapiens: Overabundant and the ultimate pest?' in *Pest or Guest: The Zoology of Overabundance*, D. Lunney, P. Eby, P. Hutchings and S. Burgin (eds), Royal Zoological Society of NSW, Mosman.

Journal of Happiness Studies (2008), special issue on hedonia, eudaimonia and wellbeing, vol. 9, Springer.

Kahneman, D., Krueger, A., Schkade, N., Schwarz, N. and Stone, A (2006) 'Would you be happier if you were richer?', *Science*, vol. 312, no. 1908.

Kasser, Tim (2002) *The High Price of Materialism*, MIT Press, Cambridge, MA.

Lea, S.E. and Webley, P. (2006) 'Money as tool, money as drug: The biological psychology of a strong incentive', *Behavioral and Brain Sciences*, vol. 29, no. 2.

Lehrer, Jonah (2006) scienceblogs.com/cortex/2006/12/post_8.php#more, accessed April 2009.

Livingston, Gordon (2004) *Too Soon Old, Too Late Smart*, Marlowe & Company, New York.

Lyubomirsky, Sonja (2008) *The How of Happiness*, Penguin Press, New York.

Lyubomirsky, Sonja, King, Laura and Diener, Ed (2005) 'The benefits of frequent positive affect: does happiness lead to success', *Psychological Bulletin*, vol. 131.

Lyubomirsky, Sonja, Sheldon, Kennon and Schkade, David (2005) 'Pursuing Happiness: The Architecture of Sustainable Change', *Review of General Psychology*, vol. 9, no. 2.

Marglin, Stephen (2008) *The Dismal Science*, Harvard University Press, Cambridge, MA.

Micklethwait, John and Wooldridge, Adrian (1996) *The Witch Doctors*, Heinemann, London.

Myers, David G. (1991) *The Pursuit of Happiness*, William Morrow, New York.

Napier, Jaime and Jost, John (2008) 'Why are Conservatives Happier than Liberals?', *Psychological Science*, vol. 19, no. 6.

Nettle, Daniel (2005) *Happiness: The Science Behind Your Smile*, Oxford University Press, Oxford.

Nickerson, C., Schwarz, N., Diener, E. and Kahneman, D. (2003) 'Zeroing on the dark side of the American dream: A closer look at the negative consequences of the goal for financial success', *Psychological Science*, vol. 14, no. 6.

Offer, Avner (2006) *The Challenge of Affluence*, Oxford University Press, Oxford.

Persaud, Raj, www.abc.net.au/rn/talks/bbing/stories/s 1537316.htm, accessed October 2009.

Prugh, Thomas, Costanza, Robert and Daly, Herman (2000) *The Local Politics of Global Sustainability*, Island Press, Washington DC.

Relationships Foundation (2007) *Thriving Lives: Which Way for Well-being?*, Cambridge, UK.

Sachs, Jeffrey (2008) *Common Wealth: Economics for a Crowded Planet*, Allen Lane, New York.

Schwartz, Barry (2004) *The Paradox of Choice*, Ecco/Harper Collins, New York.

Scitovsky, Tibor (1976) *The Joyless Economy*, Oxford University Press, New York.

Seligman, Martin E.P. (2002) *Authentic Happiness*, Random House Australia, Sydney.

Shermer, Michael (2008) *The Mind of the Market*, Times Books, New York.

Sigmund, Karl, Fehr, Ernst and Nowak, Martin (2002) 'The Economics of fair play', *Scientific American*, January.

Smith, Tom (2007) 'Job Satisfaction in the United States', www-news.uchicago.edu/releases/07/pdf/070417.jobs.pdf, accessed April 2009.

Thaler, Richard and Sunstein, Cass (2008) *Nudge: Improving Decisions about Health, Wealth and Happiness*, Yale University Press, New Haven.

Van Boven, Leaf and Gilovich, Thomas (2003) 'To do or to have: That is the question', *Journal of Personality and Social Psychology*, vol. 85, pp. 1193–202.

Veblen, Thorstein (1994) [1899] *The Theory of the Leisure Class*, Penguin Books, New York.

Vohs, Kathleen, Mead, Nicole and Goode, Miranda (2006) 'The psychological consequences of money', *Science*, vol. 314, no. 5802.

Wansink, Brian (2006) *Mindless Eating*, Bantam Books, New York.

Wolfers, Justin and Stevenson, Betsey (2008) 'Happiness Inequality in the United States', *Journal of Legal Studies*, vol. 37(S2).